UNTIL THE STARS APPEAR

From the hills
of middle America,
the enduring
power of prayer
moves mountains
in southern Africa

RANDY SPRINKLE

New Hope
Birmingham, Alabama

About the Author
Missouri native Randy Sprinkle and his wife, Nancy, have two sons: Matthew (17) and Stephen (10). The Sprinkles were Southern Baptist missionaries from 1975 to 1989 serving in the African nations of Ethiopia, Botswana, and Lesotho. They now live in Richmond, Virginia, where Randy serves as director of the Foreign Mission Board's International Prayer Strategy Office.

New Hope
P. O. Box 12065
Birmingham, AL 35202-2065

Dewey Decimal Classification: B
Subject Headings: SPRINKLE, RANDY LEON
                  SPRINKLE, NANCY ELIZABETH PHILLIPS
                  MISSIONS—ETHIOPIA
                  MISSIONS—LESOTHO
                  MISSIONARY BIOGRAPHY
                  MISSIONS, FOREIGN

Cover design by Barry Graham

ISBN: 1-56309-092-9
N944104•0496•2M2

To the
Intercessors

Till the Stars Appear

Make us Thy labourers,
Let us not dream of ever looking back
Let not our knees be feeble, hands be slack,
O make us strong to labour, strong to bear,
From the rising of the morning till the stars appear.

Make us Thy warriors,
On whom Thou canst depend to stand the brunt
Of any perilous charge on any front,
Give to us skill to handle sword and spear,
From the rising of the morning till the stars appear.

Not far from us, those stars,
Unseen as angels and yet looking through
The quiet air, the day's transparent blue.
What shall we know, and feel, and see, and hear
When the sunset colours kindle and the stars
appear?

Quoted from Amy Carmichael, *Toward Jerusalem* (Fort Washington, PA: Christian Literature Crusade, 1977), 98. Used by permission.

Contents

Acknowledgments

I write these words not at the beginning where you now read them but at the end of this endeavor. As such, I am looking back on the story, on the long process of writing that now brings this to your hand, and, most precious, on the people who made this story possible. Some of the people are named in the book. A far greater number are not. I acknowledge my indebtedness to each of them.

Because of the special involvement of two individuals in the preparation of the manuscript, I mention them here.

My wife, Nancy, has been at my side through all of our missions experiences and has been a faithful and disciplined intercessor for me and for all we have undertaken. Her place in this project was no different. From the decision to begin this effort, she took the place of intercessor. Most of the writing was done in the early morning hours, and daily she was up and praying for me as I wrote. No matter had to wait long for prayer attention because she was always nearby to talk and to take the need before our heavenly Father.

The other person I would like to thank is Dawn Phillips, who served, in essence, as my editor during the long germinal period before I had a publisher. She brought to this project the qualities and technical skills so critical in producing a book: an eye for detail and accuracy; probing questions that made me think; sensitivity to author and audience; wise yet flexible suggestions; and a keen spirit of involvement, encouragement, and prayer.

How grateful I am for these two women, one my wife, both my friends.

RLS
Missouri

Author's Note

The name Lesotho is difficult for Westerners to pronounce correctly apart from hearing it spoken. To facilitate the reading of this book, I offer the following pronunciation helps:

Le is pronounced as the *le* in *let*
so is pronounced as the word *sue*
tho is pronounced as the number *two*

    Le-so-tho
    le-sue-two

Mosotho (Mo-sue-two) is the singular for a citizen of Lesotho.

Basotho (Ba-sue-two) is the plural for the citizens of Lesotho.

Introduction

Behind and around every story are other stories. No event or sequence of events happens in a historical vacuum. This is universally acknowledged.

Not so generally known or accepted is The Story which lies behind and influences all of the stories which are our lives today.

That we might understand most fully the story told in this book, I tell again here, first—the old, old Story.

In the beginning, there was with God an only Son. The Son's name was Jesus. He was the rightful heir to the throne of the earth. A pretender to that throne, a would-be ruler named Satan, desired to usurp for himself this kingdom. Through subterfuge he led away a great army of subjects once loyal to the King and His Son, the Prince. An awful battle ensued. The rebel was victorious. The Prince was slain.

The war ended. Great mourning hung dark over the palace of the King. In the camp of the victor, wild jubilation held sway for three days.

Then the unexpected, the impossible, the unbelievable happened. The Son Prince walked again onto the field of battle. Somehow, by some great Power beyond all powers, the Prince had defeated death and the Enemy. The war hadn't really been over! But now it was.

The Prince was victorious, once and forever.

Very soon the subjects of the kingdom began to realize that the rule of the Victor Prince was to be like none other ever known, before or since. Instead of imposing His authority upon the citizens of the kingdom by force of rule, the Prince, whose new throne name was Saviour, chose a different approach. He allowed the people to choose whether or not they would follow Him.

What's more, He allowed the defeated forces and their wicked leader to roam about the kingdom for a time. They could speak to the people. They could even influence them if the people chose to listen.

1

The Prince would love His subjects with a love never before known outside the heavenly kingdom of His Father.

People flocked to the Prince. His love did conquer them. Their lives were awash in a joy they could not express. Then . . . they were devastated. The Prince announced that He was leaving for a long journey. He was going back to visit His Father. He was leaving His kingdom and its work in their hands.

They said, "You must stay with us. We need You."

He replied, "I can't stay with you any longer, but you're right. You do need Me. So, from now on, I won't be with you as I have been. I will be in You. My Spirit is going to live in you and with you. We will work together for the advance of my kingdom across this earth. Life by life, these subjects will be won to Me."

The people cried, "No! Please! Don't go. The Enemy and his evil forces are still here, and we are powerless to stand against them, let alone drive them out. Even now they are holding much of Your territory. The war is over, but skirmishes remain in every quarter. Only You have the power to resist them and displace them."

"I know that," said the Prince, "but I'm going to give My power to you. Through you the Enemy will be driven back."

How can that be? the people wondered.

"You will come to Me and to My Father, and we will be as one. I will tell you what I want you to do. I will prepare you to do it. I will give you the power you need. Just obey Me and stand in close contact with Me throughout every day."

The Prince continued, "I call this approach to life in My kingdom, *prayer*. From now until I return, we will work together in this way. We will be partners. I won't fail you. You don't fail Me."

And then He left.

From that day until this, it has continued just as He said. The way of life, the way of royal service, the way of victory is the way of prayer.

1

From the Desert to the Mountains

"**W**ell, look at that!" exclaimed a missions volunteer to several companions traveling with him through Johannesburg, South Africa.

Looking in the direction of his gaze, the missions volunteers saw a scratched and dirty four-wheel drive pickup. The pair of legs they saw protruding from beneath the front of the truck were mine.

"That looks more like the Africa we envisioned." The volunteers were in Johannesburg to board a connecting flight back to the United States. During their brief visit, they had been surprised and a bit disappointed. Everywhere on the streets of this modern African city they had seen well-dressed businessmen driving shiny automobiles. Africa wasn't supposed to be like this.

But here was a vehicle and driver looking the way Africa was supposed to look. This, they had to investigate.

"Uh, excuse me, hello."

I heard the voices and pivoted my sweaty face. As I emerged from beneath the fender, I looked into several sets of curious eyes.

"Sorry to bother you, but we saw your truck and just wondered where you're from."

My greasy hands precluded a handshake, and the press of time prevented my accepting their invitation for a lengthy visit. On another day, I would have welcomed the opportunity to talk with them. Today, however, I needed to finish my work and get back on the road.

M. G. "Bud" Fray had been watching this scene from the nearby Baptist Mission regional office. Bud was a veteran of more than 20 years of missionary service in southern Africa. Now he lived in Johannesburg and served as the associate to the area director for the Southern Baptist Foreign Mission Board. Observing this parking lot scene, his curiosity was piqued. He joined the little arc of people gathered around the front of the vehicle, exclaiming, "This looks like a prayer meeting for a truck."

Actually, prayer for the truck and the missionary under it would have been quite appropriate, both during these repairs and the difficult two-day, 1,500-kilometer drive that had just been completed.

The long trip to Johannesburg from the bush was always tiring, but this time it had been exceptionally difficult. Daily travel on the rugged bush roads had mutilated the truck's steering mechanism. Driving had become almost impossible. The logical question seemed to be: Why didn't you fix the steering before the trip? The answer was even more logical.

Homebase for our family of three was a remote village hundreds of kilometers into the Kalahari desert of northern Botswana. Auto parts stores were not a part of the landscape. So, before leaving I had radioed an order for the part. My hope was that it would be delivered to the Mission office in Johannesburg, and I could repair the truck there.

Not knowing these circumstances, Bud addressed my legs. "Hey, who's down there?"

From beneath the truck came my answer but not my body. "Hi, Bud. It's me, Randy," I said, not stopping my work.

"Well, what are you doing?"

"I'm making this truck drivable again, I hope."

Bud was a longtime friend of our family. He and his wife, Jane, had served in the bush country many years. From experience, he knew that I could have had the part airlifted to our village and saved the long trip to Johannesburg. I calculated that my answer would stir his

4

curiosity further. He had to ask the next question, "Why have you come all this way just to get a part you could have had sent to you?"

"Bud," I said, "only one thing could inspire us to drive on dirt roads through the stifling heat of the Kalahari desert with the windows rolled down and the hot wind blowing sand on us. Only one thing could keep us going until the heat and the grit become too much and Matthew begins to cry and his parents want to join him. There's only one goal important enough to make me fight this wandering, vibrating beast of a truck for two days to get here."

I paused for effect.

"Yes, Bud, there's only one reason that we would endure all of this—a vacation at the beach!"

It was spring 1982, and my wife, Nancy, and I, along with our three-year-old son Matthew, had been making plans for months. Our first visit to the beach since becoming missionaries 7 years before would be perfect.

Our appointment in 1975, during Foreign Missions Week at Glorieta, New Mexico, had formalized our calling to serve in Ethiopia. We had been excited about joining a unique team of missionaries on the mission field in Africa. These missionaries were using their skills in medicine, business, agriculture, and handcrafting to help Ethiopians better their lives. Their labors of love had opened the hearts of Ethiopians to Him Who would make all of life infinitely better. We had looked forward to laboring alongside these missionaries for the rest of our lives, little knowing that developments on two fronts were to irreversibly alter our plans.

In 1974 a Marxist group from the Ethiopian military toppled the long-reigning emperor, Haile Selassie. Eventually, one of the coup leaders, Mengistu Haile Mariam, consolidated his power and established a new Marxist-Leninist state. Almost immediately, the policies of the new government began to have a negative impact on Christian churches and missions. Increasingly, our work was hindered by a philosophy that sought to eliminate religion and any thought of God from Ethiopian life. This eventually manifested itself in the arrest and imprisonment of one of our missionaries, Sam Cannata, on false charges.

Sam's arrest set in motion an intense series of efforts to gain his release. Most important of these was the prayer that was offered not only in Addis Ababa, the capital of Ethiopia where Sam was being held, but in the United States where intercessors joined the prayer effort for his freedom.

Through a series of miraculous events, Sam was unharmed during his imprisonment which lasted less than three weeks. God had shown again the power that prayer can have over the events of this world. The lesson was not lost on the missionaries who walked through this experience, and it was not forgotten in the years and events that were to lie ahead of us.

Following this experience, it became clear that missionaries were not going to be allowed to stay in Ethiopia. Many other Christian missions had already sent out most or all of their personnel. Our own Mission reached the same reluctant conclusion. Thus, the Baptist Mission of Ethiopia became a mission in exile as the missionaries left the country and traveled to Kenya or the United States.

After many months of praying and waiting, this group of missionaries, uniquely gifted as a team, finally accepted that they would no longer labor together. The Baptist Mission of Ethiopia was being dismantled by God. Each of the missionary families began to seek His new direction for their lives. One by one they accepted other assignments in Africa.

For us, what we had thought would be a lifetime of service set in the rugged peaks and gorges of central Ethiopia lived out among proud and sturdy mountain people, was over. A lifelong sojourn suddenly had ended.

I remembered the long hours of study and struggle with the Amharic language. With more than 200 letters in its alphabet, the language is one of the most difficult in the world. Nancy and I had been investing days and nights of intense study. Our rewards were only snatches of slow progress, but they were enough. All we wanted was to be able to someday communicate with the people about God and His love.

I thought of our village, Debre Birhan (Mountain of Light), 9,000 feet up in the mountains. On bitter, cold mornings because we had no heat in our tiny mud house, we would wrap ourselves in heavy handwoven Ethiopian blankets before taking our Bibles and turning to God. We prayed for our town and its people, locked in darkness. We prayed that through us the Light of the world might shine brightly in Mountain of Light. Now we cried because we would never again walk its paths and rocky streets.

I remembered the wonderful day when I finally was able to speak in Amharic in a very simple way about Christ. With this ability, I could reach out to people not only in Debre Birhan but beyond.

Ankober was a village about an hour's drive from Debre Birhan. It had been the ancient capital of Ethiopia and, although it was small now, it was still the central village for that region of the mountains. Through discussion with neighbors, I had learned that Saturday was market day for Ankober.

All over Ethiopia each main village has a weekly market day. On market day, people come from throughout the area, spread their blankets or shawls on the ground of the central square, and sell their grain and vegetables while catching up on local news. Each Saturday I had begun to climb into our old green Land Rover and drive out to Ankober. There I would spend the day moving about the marketplace and talking with the people, sharing tracts and portions of the Gospels written in Amharic.

Communist propaganda was very intense and unending during this period, and even in this remote village, its influence had taken root. Driving slowly into Ankober each week, I would be met by gangs of children who would run along beside my truck, pointing and shouting in cadence, "CIA, CIA, CIA." I was always addressed with the curse word, *forenge*, which loosely translated means a non-Amhara of despicable foreign birth. Still, I had been overjoyed to be going to Ankober.

Finally one day on the road to Ankober, agents of the government were waiting for me. They ordered me out of the truck and began a search. Because similar situations often led to trumped-up charges, I was praying they would not find anything that could be remotely construed as subversive, or *reactionary*, a popular Communist term.

As the search progressed, a crowd gathered. I realized that the only things drawing attention were the numerous tracts and Gospel portions. After a huddled conference, the agents informed me they were confiscating a sample of all the literature.

At that moment, a thought came that demanded action. I told the men it just didn't seem fair that there were three of them and they were leaving with only one copy of each tract and booklet. I urged them to confiscate three of everything so they would each have their own copies. They found this to be an excellent idea. Then I directed their attention to key verses and paragraphs in the tracts. "You definitely must give extra attention to these," I appealed. Again, they agreed.

Finally, I glanced at the people all around us. This was the largest crowd I had ever been able to gather. The Communists were always proclaiming that this was the people's government, so I took a chance and pushed one step further. I declared that I was willing to give everyone a copy of the booklets so that they could all check out thoroughly who I was and what I stood for. To my amazement, the agents again agreed.

When I left Ankober that day, I left empty-handed. But on the paths fanning out down the mountainsides and outward in all directions from the town, people were going back to their homes and villages with hands full of the Word of God. My smile could only have been surpassed by God's.

It was good that I was smiling that day because the governor sent soldiers into the marketplace the following Saturday. The whole town watched as I was taken into custody and led away for interrogation. The result of this episode was an expulsion order that prevented me from ever returning to Ankober.

While the political situation in Ethiopia had precipitated changes in places of service for our missionaries, another situation had complicated and confused the personal search of Nancy and me for God's direction. During the winter months of the previous year, I began to notice changes in my beautiful and vivacious wife of 7 years.

It seemed that she didn't look quite the same; also her

once limitless energy was clearly waning. She had noticed that she didn't feel quite right; but Ethiopia was a place of much disease, and all of us were regularly sick with various kinds of "bugs." We had passed it off as the residual effects of several minor illnesses strung together.

But by December of that year, 1976, it was obvious that something was wrong. Our Mission doctor, Sam Cannata, recommended we travel to Nairobi, Kenya, where Nancy was hospitalized.

After numerous tests which revealed nothing, the doctors temporarily released her while additional outpatient evaluation continued. Shortly, however, she had to be rushed back to the hospital with high fever and terrible pain. Again, doctors were puzzled and found nothing.

Despite the efforts of friends in Kenya, Christmas that year was one of loneliness and darkness. Nancy's physical suffering was compounded by emotional pain as we wrestled with the events in Ethiopia. The country where we already had planted our hearts was hurting at the hands of the Communists. As the people suffered, we suffered. Slowly, although we would not talk about it, there came an eerie sense that something very awful was looming beyond the fog in which we were living.

In the deep hours of the nights as I sat with Nancy, her suffering rose and fell with her fever. I prayed the same prayers over and over for her and for Ethiopia. Glimpses emerged of something too painful to even consider. They wouldn't stay buried, and the scene was always the same. First, there were the towering mountains of our home and the deep canyons between them, canyons with cliffs like the ones behind Debre Birhan. The canyons were dangerous, rugged, dark, too wide to measure, and impossible to cross. It seemed there was a message. A vast chasm was going to be opened between Ethiopia and us: we were going to be separated from that land.

At length, when the doctors in Nairobi were still unable to diagnose Nancy's condition, we were faced with a difficult decision. The best option, the only logical choice, seemed to be to return to the United States and seek further medical help. We had long discussions about the next step. We prayed much. Finally, the day came when there was nothing else to discuss; what we had to do became clear. We bought plane tickets and returned to Ethiopia.

Nancy rested in Addis Ababa for a couple of days and then we got into our Land Rover and made the drive back over the mountains to Debre Birhan. We had fallen behind in our Amharic studies, in spite of studying together in the hospital and in our room. Over the next few months, we adjusted our schedules to accommodate Nancy's declining health. Although she had spent most of her time in bed, we completed our Amharic language studies and graduated.

On weekends I had been traveling into the Menjir region east of Addis Ababa, moving our things and readying a house for our first real home in Ethiopia. On graduation day, we packed the Land Rover and said our good-byes. The missionaries from other groups, who had been strangers only a year earlier, were now family: the doctor from Kansas, the dentist from England, the agriculturist from Iowa, the translator from Ireland, the doctor and teacher from Scotland, the nurse from California, and our language teacher from Canada.

Through tears, we imagined ourselves walking with the Ethiopians through all that this communistic scourge was bringing upon them. They must know that Christ would never leave them and, somehow, neither would we. Even though our eyes were finally dry as we drove out of Debre Birhan, we still weren't seeing.

We went first for supplies to Addis Ababa where Sam was waiting for us. He had come to Debre Birhan several times over the past months to examine Nancy and draw blood. Unknown to us, he also had been searching his medical books, looking for some clue to the mysterious disease that was ravaging her body.

As we sat together in the guest room the Mission had prepared for us, Sam began to lay out the situation as he saw it. He was tentative and not at all his normally positive and upbeat self. Later, his wife, Ginny, would tell us that he had been agonizing for days over this meeting. He never mentioned a diagnosis, although in response to questions by our fellow missionaries in an earlier prayer meeting, he had told them that he suspected that Nancy had contracted an incurable disease called systemic lupus erythematosus. He told us the situation was serious. He wasn't sure exactly what was at work, but it definitely was critical.

Although we were listening, we weren't hearing. We suggested other possibilities. "Isn't there something else we could try here?" Finally, he said quietly but directly, "Either you're going to have to make immediate plans to get Nancy back to the States, or you're going to have to make plans to bury her here."

I have no recollection of anything else that was said in that meeting. The fog had finally been swept away. That thing which had been looming large, but unacknowledged, now exploded upon us like a bomb. The rest of our short days in Ethiopia are a blur.

Later at Missouri Baptist Hospital in St. Louis, specialists and their sophisticated tests confirmed what the bush doctor had already told our colleagues. Nancy had lupus.

The first weeks were tense. Nancy received steroid treatment. We waited to see if the disease would be slowed. Lupus, we learned, is a disease of the body's immune system. When the immune system is damaged, the body begins to destroy itself. Medical researchers have been unable to find either the cause or a cure for the disease. Steroids are used to try to suppress the disease into remission.

While Nancy fought for her life in St. Louis, Sam was in prison in Ethiopia. Our praying became, at the same time, both enlarged and reduced. Time with God was almost constant. The scope of our praying narrowed to focus primarily on these two people. Our constant plea was for their release. Soon one was released, and we rejoiced and praised God for His graciousness to Sam. But the other wasn't, and we were thrust into the mystery of unanswered prayer.

Through the struggle of faith and understanding that would lie ahead, we comprehended that what seems to be unanswered prayer often isn't really that at all. Instead, it is prayer answered out of God's infinite wisdom, but viewed through our finite eyes.

Nancy wasn't released from her bondage, but it was not

because His grace was any less toward her. Prayer doesn't help us to gain what we desire according to our understanding but to gain what He desires. We can trust that His purposes and intents are best, as are His ways of achieving them. Not only is the Lamb worthy, He is trustworthy.

The long months of medical leave were at first dominated by Nancy's health and the immediate concerns that went with it. Slowly, as the disease moved into remission, we recognized that rising within us was something both powerful and consuming. Our call to ministry in Africa was flaming up within us again. While this was cause for hope and some brief tastes of happiness, it also intensified our pain. The weight of a terrible dilemma pressed down upon us. The Foreign Mission Board's medical consultant, while being supportive, informed us that because of the prognosis for lupus patients we would have to resign from foreign mission service. The letter had already arrived from the Board reluctantly requesting a formal letter of resignation from us. The conflicting directions of two authorities, one heavenly, one earthly, now met head-on.

Then, in a strange twist of irony, Sam Cannata came into our lives again. While we struggled to reconcile God's clear call upon our lives with the circumstances that seemed to preclude any realization of that call, Sam came to visit us in Fargo, North Dakota. A year before we had invited Sam and Ginny to spend part of their next furlough with us and lead a weekend missions conference at Temple Baptist Church where we were members. Coincidentally, it was during these same days that we were trying to come to an honest way of writing a letter of resignation that we knew was contrary to God's will. Those few days of talking to Sam and wrestling with the question brought this word: "Write the letter of resignation because you have to. But also state what you know to be true: God does not intend for you to remain in the States but rather to return to Africa and continue your ministry."

Sam left after the conference, and we wrote the letter. As we mailed it, we were placing it not just in a mailbox but in God's hands. Reflecting later in Africa, we realized it was just like God Who loves to do special things for His beloved children. An anguished friend had borne the news that effectively ended our missions careers in Ethiopia. Then God brought him to the other side of the world and gave him the privilege of bringing the word of rebirth to those careers. The Foreign Mission Board refused our resignation and instead cleared us to return to Africa.

The lesson of this difficult experience was clear. Circumstances are not powerful enough to thwart God's desires if—and this is the condition that determines the result—one seeks from Him an understanding of His will and then perseveres in faithful prayer until His infinite power is brought to bear. We had thought that the only way His will could be done was for Nancy to be healed. Instead, He showed in prayer that He had other purposes beyond just mission service that only could be realized if He were allowed to work as He chose. He seemed to be saying, *There's much more here than you see, but I'll give you what you need to walk this path. It's called grace.* When we grasped that, our assent was easy.

During this period we also recognized two themes which have been dominant in the rest of our lives. They are the rich experiences of prayer and pain.

Since Ethiopia remained closed to us because of limited medical facilities, we found ourselves in the remote desert village of Maun in northwestern Botswana working among the Batswana people. The conditions were not pleasurable or easy. In the Kalahari desert, there is really not a winter as we are used to it. This wasn't so bad, but such a luxury meant that summer was six months long with temperatures that sometimes reached 120 degrees. Our home was basic, but comfortable. Because we didn't have electricity, we could not have air-conditioning or even fans. Our water came from a nearby river where we always had to be on guard for crocodiles and snakes.

The sand and the dust constantly bothered us, but the greatest difficulty was the numbing fatigue that settled upon us during the long summer months. Eventually every step would become a conscious effort. Each night we would fall exhausted into bed, only to fight the mosquitoes and the heat for a few hours of rest. In spite of this, we thrived. Nancy was careful and disciplined, and her health was excellent. We had acquired a good command of the Setswana language, and God was communicating His message of love through us to these gentle desert people. Working with another missionary couple, Pete and Becky Baer, we saw people coming to Christ from the very beginning. One by one, we began to establish churches in and around Maun.

After 2½ years in Botswana, we were in need of, and excited about, our first real getaway in years. That's when the steering on our truck went awry, and I could not get the part to repair it. Our long-anticipated vacation was impossible. Then came the idea. We had to travel through Johannesburg on our way to the Indian Ocean city of Durban anyway. Why not send a radio message to missionaries in Johannesburg asking them to order the part? We would stop there just long enough to make the repair. Then we could be on our way. All I had to do was somehow drive this darting and unpredictable truck for two days across the Kalahari desert and on into Johannesburg.

As we pulled into the parking lot of the Baptist Mission office in Johannesburg, relief swept over us. We had made it. A brief repair and then we could concentrate on the sole purpose of our trip. We were going to enjoy a wonderful time of rest and fun together as a family. We never suspected that God had another, more far-reaching, purpose for this trip. While we were looking to the beach, He was looking toward the mountains—the mountains of Lesotho.

2

The Call

Almost everyone in Texas was complaining about the heat during the summer of 1986. Each day the temperature was in the high 90s and sometimes reached 100 degrees. We listened, but we didn't say much. After the scorching heat of the African desert, we were enjoying the respite.

We were in Fort Worth for furlough after completing our term of service in Botswana. I was doing post-graduate study in missions and cross-cultural studies at Southwestern Baptist Theological Seminary. We were praying that this time of study during furlough would equip us for more effective service.

The year 1986 was set apart as a special one for our family: our second child, Stephen, had been born in January. Nancy had come through her pregnancy with a minimum of difficulties and was continuing to do well as we moved into the summer months. The dangerous period after delivery had passed without a relapse of her lupus, and Stephen was a healthy and cheerful baby. We were a happy family, with the difficulties characterizing our early years of missionary service now apparently behind us. With eagerness, we anticipated the remaining months of our furlough and our return to the field. Only one unresolved issue marred our otherwise placid summer—which field?

Months earlier I had been working at my desk in our air-conditioned furlough home when the telephone rang. As I got up to answer the phone I thought, *It's probably a church calling to invite me to speak*. As it rang again, I wondered where my calendar was. With the third ring, I was moving into the kitchen and approaching the phone. As my hand reached for it, I could not know that this wonderful period of tranquility and happiness for my family would end in only a few milliseconds.

I thought I was simply answering the phone. I didn't sense anything significant at all. I certainly didn't notice all of heaven was watching! Actually the lifting of the handpiece was like the moving of a lever opening an enormous floodgate. Slowly the gears began to turn and do their work. Almost imperceptibly, the gate started to open. Eventually, it would grow into a great current that would at first be welcome and a blessing; but, it would bring with it a pressure and a power that would seek to sweep us away. There would be a desperate struggle.

At the time, I didn't see any of this. I thought only that the phone was ringing. Later, much later, I would realize it hadn't been simply the sound of a telephone. It was the sound of a shot, a shot across the bow of the Enemy, the first shot of what was to become a war. Then I didn't understand that. Calmly, I picked up the phone and offered, "Hello?"

The caller was Davis Saunders of the Foreign Mission Board in Richmond, Virginia. Davis was then area director for all Southern Baptist missions in eastern and southern Africa. A former US marine, he was a big man, diligent and hardworking. He and his wife, Mary, had been some of our pioneering missionaries in the early years of Baptist work in East Africa. He was a man who wasted little in action or speech.

He had walked with us through the difficult years. When our medical situation seemed to preclude any future in African missions, he had listened as we shared a different word—a word that said, "Trust Me and I will do it."

Wisely, Davis had not responded with, "I'm sorry, but it's impossible." He had said, "All right, if this is of God, I'll join you in praying and waiting for Him to work out a way."

16

Faithfully he had, and he had rejoiced with us when God miraculously opened again the way to Africa for us. It was a trusted friend and prayer partner who called that day.

The story Davis began to share was one of another answer to prayer. For years, prayers had been lifted for the opening of one of the countries in his region where Southern Baptists had no missions work. In answer to these pleas, God had worked in that land, and now Davis reported that the country was being opened to missionaries by its government. He had been seeking direction regarding who God desired to send in to establish the new Mission. He was led to us.

His request was simple and direct. Were we open to leaving Botswana? If so, would we begin to ask God's direction regarding our transferring to the island nation of Madagascar?

My mind spun. Nothing had prepared us for this. As we talked, my thoughts raced back over all the effort that had gone into learning the culture and language of Botswana. I lamented the settledness and effectiveness that would be left behind. I knew how much time and toil would be required to replicate this in the new environment of Madagascar. A reasonable response seemed obvious, "No, that doesn't make sense."

But, I trusted Davis' spiritual life. Prayer had taught me that sometimes what doesn't seem right and reasonable to our human wisdom is just that in God's wisdom. No, we wouldn't move on Davis' word alone, but we were willing to open our lives to match the openness of the path now laid before us. We were under no illusions. We knew what we were about to lay before the Lord could be taken away if He so chose. Our answer matched the direct simplicity of the question before us. "Yes, we'll seek His direction."

God's nearness permeated the weeks that followed. We spent time early each day in solitary prayer with Him. Throughout the rest of the day He engaged our minds and spirits in this journey.

Whenever the time we spend in seeking God's will is lengthy, we naturally conclude that He is reluctant to answer. This is never true. His great desire is for us to know and do His will. The time we spend in knowing His will is time in which He renews and purifies our commitment to Jesus as Lord. Often in our lives much accumulates that makes His will more difficult to discern. Moreover, if we did know God's divine will from the beginning, these same weights and hindrances might impede our doing His will.

He answers our searching petitions with His Spirit's searching power. He reveals hidden sins. He illuminates areas of our lives that have grown unwilling. He offers release from burdens. He highlights our rationalizations for the rebellions that they are. And, at each turn, He waits for our agreement, our confession, and our submission. Instead of seeing His will, we see ourselves. It must be this way or else we would be left to do His work with our power—and that is impossible.

He works. He waits. He guides us forward. He readies us to receive His will. He empowers us to do it. It's like the path to a lookout point. Only one way leads to the glorious and unobstructed view. We journey into the knowledge of His will. We reach our destination when—purified, focused, and undivided—from the altar of our hearts rises a quiet and liberated, "Thy will be done." From that moment until His word arrives, only praise and joy abound.

After a period of weeks, it was our turn to talk with Davis.

As I wrote him, I mentally moved through the past weeks of private walk with God. My answer for Davis was not as clear-cut as he would have liked, but He would not be surprised. I knew that. On other occasions we had sat together and reminisced about our career and the unusual turns that it had taken. He had said, "Well, I know one thing. With you two, it's never going to be simple or dull." I prefaced my answer by recalling those words.

I gave him the good news first. It was clear that God intended for us to transfer from Botswana and begin work in a new place. But, I stated, we had an equally strong conviction that it was not to be Madagascar. Davis had a dilemma. Not only did he have an open country with no missionaries to send in, he now had a family that didn't want to go back to its field. His problems were multiplying.

Then, to complicate things further, I said that through the last days of our time with God regarding this question, one word had begun to predominate. It was the name of a country: Lesotho. As we prayed about other things: Lesotho. As we read our Bibles: Lesotho. As we went about daily tasks with no seeming connection to missions: Lesotho. At every turn, whispered into our consciousness, unmistakably: "The country of Lesotho." We came to believe, also undeniably, that the voice was God's.

I remembered that all efforts over past years to secure openings to Lesotho had met closed doors. Contacts with government officials in the country had always been unproductive. Now I put before Davis the conviction that it was time to knock again. We would wait and pray. The next step was his.

In the walk that is the Christian life come times when plans—good plans—come up against possibilities that are not on our agenda. These are decision times. They may even be momentous times. In these times, a rigid adherence to program will rule out consideration of other options. Davis Saunders was a man of organization and planning; but he had learned that God has His own timetable and our surrender to His Lordship must always include flexibility.

Lesotho wasn't on the game plan at the Foreign Mission Board, but it didn't take long to draw a new plan. A call by Davis to James Westmoreland, his associate in Johannesburg, soon put James on the road to Lesotho. His assignment was to knock again on the door of that nation. However, when he arrived, he didn't have to knock. The door was already open. God's time had come.

In our letter to Davis, I had addressed all the pertinent points regarding our understanding of God's will concerning Lesotho. I didn't include, though, the most significant single piece that had brought the whole picture into focus. It was a snippet of mental movie film, and it had been projected repeatedly on the screens of our minds. The film had only one scene.

In it I saw a relaxed father driving easily, confidently, a work-worn pickup truck with new steering, south out of Johannesburg, South Africa. On the seat of the truck with him was his wife, animated and happy, reaching across the back of the seat to touch and say to him, silently, "I love you." Between them was a little boy full of a hundred excited questions, trying to ask them all in one unbroken string. The travelers suddenly noticed a range of gray, dark mountains outlining the western horizon. They were massive and, at once, both fascinating and troubling. In conversation, the couple wondered about these mountains, what they were called, who lived there. Finally, they took out a map. The man checked their position and announced, "Nancy, that's Lesotho." They shared for a few moments the little they knew about the country. Then the map and Lesotho were put away. The family continued traveling toward Durban and the beach . . . and the future they had just glimpsed but failed to recognize.

The rest of the film was blank. The scene had stood alone, suspended in time, until the telephone rang that day in a mission house in Texas. Suddenly the film clip assumed pivotal importance.

While we prayed and waited for the Foreign Mission Board to inquire of the government officials in Lesotho, we did some investigating of Lesotho on our own. We learned it is one of the smallest, yet most unique, countries in the world. Because it is tiny and completely surrounded by the larger and more well-known Republic of South Africa, Lesotho is generally unknown in most of the Western world.

Its mountains are the dominant physical feature. High mountainous terrain often conjures images of Switzerland and Nepal; but, Lesotho owns the distinction of being the nation with the highest average elevation in the world. Its lowlands are nearly one mile high. This, coupled with Lesotho's monarchical form of government, has earned it the unofficial title of the Mountain Kingdom.

Ethnically, the people of Lesotho share a uniformity rare for African nations. The vast majority have a common tribal ancestry and are united in loyalty to the royal house of King Moshoeshoe. They also share the Sesotho language.

Moshoeshoe is one of the most famous and well-respected chiefs in African history. He was a minor chief in the early 1820s when the Zulu warrior chief, Shaka,

20

began his military campaigns that brought turmoil and displacement to the people of southern Africa. In response, Moshoeshoe moved his people into the mountains of what is now Lesotho for protection. As other refugees fled into the area, he displayed his wisdom by assimilating them into his tribe. Thus, over time, he built a mighty nation. Moshoeshoe's military and diplomatic skills were far ahead of their time. These, linked with the natural defenses of the mountains, enabled him to successfully defend the land against the Zulus. Later, he also defeated the Boers and the British.

Finally, though, Moshoeshoe realized he could not stand forever against the growing power of the South Africans. In 1868 his request of the queen of England was granted, and Lesotho (then Basutoland) became part of the British Empire. On the surface this would seem a great loss, but actually it was the only realistic option. Now potential enemies would be attacking not Lesotho but the British Empire. In giving up sovereignty, Moshoeshoe had saved his nation.

Nearly a century later, in 1966, the country would regain its independence from Great Britain and become the modern nation of Lesotho.

Christian missions have also played an important role throughout the history of Lesotho. In 1833 Protestant missionaries of the Paris Evangelical Missionary Society met Moshoeshoe and were given permission to take up residence in his country. In 1862 Catholic missionaries arrived and were allowed to live and work in another part of the land. Through the years these missions provided education and religious influence, as well as invaluable insight and advice to Moshoeshoe as he dealt with the Europeans. One of the Paris missionaries, Eugene Casalis, served, in essence, as foreign minister for Lesotho from 1837 to 1855.

The 1.5 million citizens of modern-day Lesotho labor under difficult circumstances. Because the country contains very few natural resources, the development of business and industry has been a struggle. In recent decades, the majority of the able-bodied men have worked in the mines of South Africa. The work is hard and dangerous, but the Basotho men have become recognized as out-standing miners. Their wages provide the monetary basis for the national economy back home, but at a high cost. The men are gone for long periods of time, sometimes as long as two years. This absence of husbands and fathers has put the traditional culture under severe strain.

In 1986 a coup was staged in the capital city of Maseru. The prime minister was removed and the constitution was suspended. Since that time, slowly moving negotiations to return the country to some form of representative government finally resulted in national elections in 1993.

But in the summer of 1986 at the Foreign Mission Board, things were moving anything but slowly. James Westmoreland's report with its positive findings had arrived. Davis Saunders was weighing these developments against the multitude of other options and possibilities in the region. The problem of an open Madagascar without missionaries to assign had been resolved by God's preparing another missionary family in East Africa to go there. As Davis deliberated, we prayed. Finally, he knew what he would present to the Foreign Mission Board's fall meeting in October.

For us, the summer was spent waiting and thinking about those mountains. Would we only see them from afar? Or was a way really being prepared for us to serve there? Davis' word to us immediately after the Board's meeting answered that question. "Your transfer and the establishment of a Baptist Mission in Lesotho have been approved."

We were going in.

3

I Will Do a New Thing

I stood under a tree on the campus of Southwestern Baptist Theological Seminary in Fort Worth, Texas, watching Gene Meachem's eyes fill with tears. He'd heard our exciting news about Lesotho, and he knew some background I needed to know. In a voice choked with emotion, he was trying to tell me a story about an airplane flight, but I recognized that it was really a story about God, His love, and a little country called Lesotho.

The midsize commuter plane taxied for takeoff from the airport in Umtata, Transkei. Beside his wife, missionary Gene Meachem sat, lost in a swirl of thoughts as the plane began accelerating down the runway. They had finished their first term of service in Transkei, a South African homeland, and were beginning their furlough journey home to the States. Packing and closing up always require much work, but the real difficulty in leaving on furlough is saying good-bye to the churches, the leaders, friends, and especially those who were without Christ when you came and now are brothers and sisters in the wonderful family of God. The Meachems had said their good-byes. It had been hard.

The aircraft engines roared as the plane gathered speed. The missionaries grieved, for in lifting off, their physical contact with the country and the people they loved would be broken. Gene's thoughts washed over him in a flood of emotion. This break with the Transkei people might be much longer than just a furlough. The Meachems were unsure if they would be returning after furlough.

Takeoff accomplished, the plane climbed out, turning north and heading for Johannesburg. There a jumbo jet waited to carry them homeward. Gene broke his troubled thoughts long enough to glance at his wife. She was turned, peering out the little porthole window of the plane. An intensity about her downward gaze seized Gene's attention. At first, he thought she was trying to capture a last glimpse of Transkei, but Transkei was already far behind them. They were over some other country. What was she thinking? Her eyes were filling with tears.

Gene reached to comfort his wife. She was probably overcome by the realization that they might never see Transkei and its people again. His hand moved to console her, his voice reassuring. Her response surprised him. "No, Gene, that's not it. Look down there."

Leaning across her, he saw, undulating below in every direction, what seemed to be giant waves on a stormy, dark sea. Gene knew the flight path. The aircraft couldn't be over the ocean. These were mountains—towering mountains—with steep, rocky valleys between them.

"Gene," she said. "That's Lesotho. I'm just so burdened for that country and its people. We've got to pray for them."

The stares of the passengers nearby went unnoticed as the two missionaries bowed their heads. God's love for Lesotho had been seeking a channel for expression. It found two, and a beautiful picture of intercession emerged. Spread below was the nation, the focus of God's desire. Spread above was heaven. And here, suspended between the two, was a couple alert enough to hear His summons and willing enough to respond. With reverence, they said, "Our Father." The vast expanse was bridged and heaven and earth were joined. His great love seeking a fresh opportunity in the Mountain Kingdom was breaking free.

As Gene finished telling me his story, I understood more clearly what Charles Wesley had grasped a century earlier: "God does nothing but in answer to prayer."

Prayer is vital to God's progressing, advancing work on earth. Nancy and I had just completed a period of praying that had resulted in a step forward for Christ's kingdom and for us. Before us, though, had come other pray-ers. How many? We could not know; but, from an unlikely setting, an airplane high above the earth, came assurance that, though hidden to us in the present, other intercessors had been there in the past. Their uplifted faces had sought God for Lesotho and their requests were not in vain, not forgotten, not unheard. Their prayers lived on.

We comprehended this truth. A second encounter in Texas solidified it for us forever.

A wedding is always a special and memorable time. For missionaries, an MK (missionaries' kid) wedding is especially wonderful. Not only do we celebrate the joining of two lives, but we celebrate the renewal of friendships with other missionaries. Furloughing, as well as former, missionaries come together, and the wedding becomes a family reunion of sorts. Nancy and I were enjoying one such wedding when we saw our old friends, Bud and Jane Fray, coming through the crowd at the reception. We had barely exchanged hugs before they excitedly and joyfully began talking about the opening of Lesotho. For them, the happiness of the wedding was multiplied by the joy they felt over our going to Lesotho. We were sharing in two new beginnings.

They had been furloughing in Arkansas and knew nothing of developments regarding Lesotho. One day they received their state Baptist paper, and as they glanced through it, their attention was caught by the names Randy and Nancy Sprinkle and Lesotho. With a mixture of jubilation and disbelief, they read and reread the article. As they related their story, we realized we were standing in the presence of two more whom God had used to prepare the way in Lesotho.

During their years in Johannesburg, the Frays had become concerned for Lesotho and its people. Their concern spawned prayer, and eventually Bud made a survey trip to the country to test the waters for the Foreign Mission Board. He met with various government officials in the Interior and Immigration departments. He spoke with agencies and organizations that assisted with aid and development. He visited with other religious entities. At each stop he probed for some need our missionaries might meet, an entrance to Lesotho. He found none.

So he returned to Johannesburg, and he and Jane had kept working at gaining an entrance to Lesotho. They worked with God. They prayed.

The excitement of the setting matched ours as we talked with these pray-ers. We stood amazed and humbled as they rejoiced: "For seven years we've been praying for Lesotho. Now the answer has come!"

It is my conviction that there are many other intercessors for Lesotho that I have never met. Perhaps some of these were Basotho, citizens of Lesotho, living in the country and praying for their own people. Only God knows how much prayer went into setting the stage for that dramatic scene in the skies above Lesotho.

On the other side of the world, God could work the next phase of the plan that resulted in the Foreign Mission Board's October 1986 decision to transfer us to Lesotho. The flow of God's purpose was evident. He was at work, and through prayer we were working with Him. We were reaching out in love to people without Christ. We were seeking ways to express that love. In our powerlessness to open a way of expression, we were coming to Him who has almighty power. We were joining with God. The next step in our preparation was to reveal just how great this joining in prayer was to be.

Normally, when new missionaries go into a country, all the preparations for their arrival and their first year of service are made by the missionaries already there.

For example, in 1976 when we arrived as first-term missionaries in Ethiopia, we were met at the airport by a welcoming party of all the Baptist missionaries who could get there. They helped us through Customs and Immigration. They loaded our bags into a waiting station wagon and drove us to an apartment they had furnished and readied for our arrival. Dishes were in the cupboard; food was in the refrigerator. Meal invitations from our new colleagues awaited us. Our co-workers did everything they could to make our initial transition smooth and positive.

Once we were rested and our body clocks reset, the Mission business manager began to take us around the capital city. We learned where to shop. We learned which areas were safe and which weren't. He helped us get registered with the government and take care of details such as driver's licenses and bank accounts. We visited some of our existing mission stations and learned about the country and our missions work. We had the opportunity to work with the people before moving to the long task of language study.

At the language school, we found a qualified teacher waiting for us. There were nationals to work with us daily on pronunciation and speaking drills. Other missionaries were always available to listen and answer questions. They also were there just to be friends.

Everything possible had been taken care of for us before our plane even landed in the country.

In moving to Lesotho, however, there would be no missionaries from our denomination already there to make these preparations. We would have to do all the planning we could before arrival and then take care of our own needs as we faced them. As we began to think through this preparation process, we drew on past experience for insight. How could we best move alone into a strange country and establish our home and the Mission? As we planned, we were encouraged. Our years of missions experience were like notebooks filled in a field laboratory. Our library of missiological knowledge and theory, read and reflected upon, had been tested and integrated into our day-by-day ministry in foreign cultures. We didn't realize until this time that God had prepared in us a strong reference library on which we now freely drew. We saw in our past God's preparation for the next step.

We were encouraged in every area of our planning but one—the most important one. What direction should we take in starting our actual missions work in Lesotho? What approach would best suit the unique cultural, political, and spiritual conditions we would find there? How should we begin to build this new Mission?

Years before, along a dirt airstrip in the Kalahari desert, I had built a large steel aircraft hangar to house the plane I operated for our Mission. The actual building was designed by engineers who were knowledgeable and experienced in their field. It was constructed of the best materials and assembled according to detailed plans. It stood strong and sturdy against the winds of the desert storms.

But, its usefulness and its enduring character did not depend solely on its components or design. It depended on something very common and easily forgotten in the excitement of raising a large and impressive structure. Great pains had been taken to put down a right foundation. All that was then built upon it could be straight and strong. The building could be exactly what its designers intended it to be.

From experience in other countries, Nancy and I had developed a principle which said, "The way you get in is the way you go on." It reminded us that our future options, and even our effectiveness, would be determined by the decisions we were making in the present.

We had served in Missions handcuffed by unwise past decisions. We knew how much a Mission's potential is affected by what transpires in its early life. We were determined that before the Baptist Mission of Lesotho even existed, a solid foundation would be laid by God.

As we reviewed our central concern for mission strategy, we realized that we knew how to design a strategy that would have the strength and the flexibility to serve us and those who would follow. We knew what components the Mission's structure must have for optimum effectiveness. What we didn't understand was what kind of foundation God wanted to lay down under it. The gravity of the situation drove us to prayer. It was there that we came to understand.

The days of praying became weeks. Each morning started with time in God's presence, seeking His guidance and listening for His response. The conviction grew in us that God had a purpose in this burden that was upon us, this longing for specific direction. We sought it that, like S. D. Gordon, we might "make that purpose our prayer."

The heart of our praying was, "You, Lord, have chosen this country at this time in history to do a new work.

Through the prayers of willing servants, You have prepared the people and opened the way. You have called us out of our equipping years and set us to this task. Now we are about to take up the actual work. How are we to begin?

"We know our beginnings either will enhance or hinder the work of our colleagues who will join us and those who will come after we are gone. A Mission's history—a history that we pray will be long and blessed with much fruit—is about to begin. How is it to begin?

"Upon what foundation do You want to build Your work in this new Mission?"

November arrived bringing a new crispness to the air. The winds were distinctly cooler. We had lived in Texas before and knew what this meant. In a few weeks blue northers, winter storms, would swoop down from the panhandle and blast the seminary campus and all of northern Texas. It was a chilling thought.

Inside our furlough home, though, our thoughts and lives were warm. We were experiencing God in a fresh way. In these weeks of focused, ardent petition, God had renewed us. We had struggled and enjoyed at the same time. We hadn't received the answer to our prayers yet, but we were more confident. God was doing something. He would show it. We would join Him.

The morning of November 4, 1986, dawned like any other. I arose early and went to the bedroom we had converted to a study. Taking my Bible, I sat down at my desk and prepared to pray. After a time of reading, I bowed. As I stilled and focused my mind, I began to speak to the One Who loved me and looked forward to this time more than I did. I brought to Him friends with hurts and situations that needed His intervention. I prayed for my wife and her health. I brought to Him our two sons, the new baby and the second-grader who wasn't too sure about leaving Botswana and his pets to go to a strange place that was cold. And I prayed for this new Mission and its direction.

In the days that had gone before, the pattern of my praying had been generally the same. Times of speaking to God were interspersed with silent moments in which I just sat before Him. This morning began the same. It was soon apparent, though, that it was to end very differently. As I prayed for the Mission and its beginnings, I realized that God was ready to speak. He was addressing this question that dominated our thinking and our praying. He was answering.

He told me, *I have prepared the way for this day through the prayers of many people over many years. The country has been opened to you through prayer. Now, I want to build this Mission and its ministry upon the same foundation, upon a foundation of prayer. Everything that you do, every decision, and every advance will be undergirded by prayer. Then I will build this Mission.*

I thought He was directing this to Nancy and me. I responded, *Of course. Yes. We will seek Your will and blessing at every turn. We will commit, with our colleagues, to giving prayer first place in the life of this Mission.*

Yes, He answered, *but more than that, I have others that I want to link with you in this.*

Wonderful! I thought. Then I prayed about how this might manifest itself. *Could there be a church somewhere that would be willing to commit itself to Lesotho, to take intercessory responsibility with us for the advance of the gospel in that land?*

Even as I brought it to Him, He answered, *No, it's not just a church.*

Could it be a whole association of churches? I prayed. *That would be impossible. How could I work from the other side of the world with a group of churches? How could I communicate with that many people?* Without realizing it, I was weighing feasibility while God was trying to give a vision.

Before I could think and express my reservations, He answered, *No, it's not an association.*

Now I was aware of a surge. I was being caught up. My boundaries, limitations, and practical considerations were suddenly fading away. And then I knew. It burst out of me, *It's a state! It is a whole state.*

There was no thought that hour of how it could be, only, *It is to be.*

His quiet, affirming word was, *It is a state. I have chosen and readied an entire state convention for this task.*

God was assigning not just two to Lesotho, He was assigning thousands.

I was awed that day by the magnitude of what He revealed. I still am.

4

Show Me

Alberta Gilpin leaned back in her desk chair. She felt wonderful. Her eyes moved over the many objects from foreign lands decorating her office in the Missouri Baptist Building in Jefferson City, Missouri. She thought of the missionaries in those countries and the people to whom they ministered. For nearly 20 years she had served Christ and missions through the Missouri Woman's Missionary Union (WMU). As director, she led the work of training and missions education for WMU in the state. Now, as 1986 was ending, she reviewed the detailed plans she and her staff had prepared for the new year, plans which were thorough, complete, and funded. Just days before, the annual state Baptist convention had approved the budget.

Yes, she thought to herself as she laid the papers on her desk, *I feel great. Everything is ready. There should be no surprises in 1987.*

In Fort Worth I was still staggered by God's revelation of His prayer plan for Lesotho. The demands of the day beckoned me, but I resisted their summons. I did not want to leave this place of prayer where God had met me. I didn't want the moment to end. But, of course, it had to. Every meeting with God, every word from Him must be followed by life back in the world, life that is different because of God's speaking into it. Reluctantly, I opened my eyes. I was a furloughing missionary again. Glancing around the room, I realized everything looked the same. Physically, it was. Actually, however, everything in our lives had begun to change. It changed because God had just given new direction; and, it changed because we had responded with submission to His direction.

Divine direction, coupled with human obedience, always brings repercussions that pervade and affect every area of our lives, sometimes subtly, sometimes radically. The first of those effects had come even before that morning's prayertime was completed. I knew, as I responded to God's revealing of His plan, if He intended for a state to shoulder this responsibility, then He had already made much preparation in that state. Our question was not, *Which state should we choose?* but rather, *Which state have You chosen?* The first practical act of obedience was the confession, "It doesn't matter whom You've chosen. I'll go anywhere, to any state, to meet Your people and work with them to bring this grand plan to pass."

As Nancy and I talked about what God had just shown, we began focusing on the practical steps that would be necessary to see His plan implemented. We determined the first priority was to locate the state. By midmorning we had decided that a call to the intercessory prayer office at the Foreign Mission Board would be a logical first step.

Minette Drumwright is the widow of my former dean at Southwestern Seminary, Huber Drumwright. She was called to the Foreign Mission Board as a special assistant for intercessory prayer. We had not known each other during our earlier seminary years, but had since become friends. She would take seriously this word I was going to share with her. Prayerfully, I called Richmond. I laid before Minette this freshly given vision of prayer as practical mission strategy: God wanted to use, through prayer, a state of Baptists to begin a Mission in a new country. I sensed as she listened that she was being captivated by the idea.

"We," she interjected, "have never done anything like this before in Southern Baptist missions life."

As we talked, she was glimpsing the vastness of possibility which concerted prayer lays open before God. When I finished the story, the reply in her soft southern accent was measured, and yet heartfelt, "This is marvelous."

"Minette," I continued, "I didn't call just to share this with you. I need your help. Our conviction is that God has already prepared a state convention somewhere for this commitment; but, we've been out of the country for several years, and we don't have any idea which states might even be possibilities. Can you help?"

There was a silent pause on the line, and then she responded. "As you asked me that, I realized something that I hadn't recognized before. From the moment you began sharing this story with me, there has been at the back of my mind a state."

Minette travels across the Southern Baptist Convention speaking and meeting with leaders to encourage increased prayer involvement. I was counting on her having insight that would point us in the right direction. She paused again, seeking, it seemed, assurance that what she was about to say was also what God was saying.

With care, she said, "There is only one state that I know of that might be ready to catch the vision for a venture of this magnitude."

Not only had God prepared a state, He had prepared this woman as the guide to the state. Earlier in the year, Minette had been in Missouri at WMU conferences. She had learned of changes that had been implemented in Missouri WMU in 1984. These changes had sprung out of the predawn prayertimes of Alberta Gilpin. Each associational WMU was reorganized to include a prayer coordinator. Local churches were encouraged to have prayer coordinators as well. Especially significant was the birth of a monthly missions prayer guide. These guides were prepared by a state WMU prayer coordinator and sent to each association for copying and distribution. God had already established a prayer network of WMU women. Not only were they furthering His will around the world, but He had begun to teach and prepare these intercessors for an even greater responsibility that was to come.

As Minette spoke, I remembered my commitment of that morning to gladly accept any state God chose. As she continued, my mind raced across the US, trying to imagine which state it might be. As I pondered the possibilities, I realized that I had no hint as to whom God had prepared.

I asked eagerly, "Tell me, which state is it?"

Minette answered, "It's Missouri."

Now it was my turn to pause, to leave the conversation hanging. Missouri. Could Minette know? No, that was impossible. She knew us only from our Texas ties on furloughs. I was nearly overcome by emotion. Now I understood the significance of the first step of obedience God had led me to take that morning. I realized why it was so important that I be willing to go anywhere He chose. As in the old hymn, "Wherever He Leads I'll Go," an honestly expressed "wherever" is a renewed commitment to His Lordship.

I also wondered how, just a moment before, I could have had no idea which state He would select and the next I knew. No wondering, no questioning, I knew. The answer was God. It was His word spoken unmistakably.

This wasn't why the answer was so emotional to me, however. Minette couldn't have known the significance of her answer. She didn't know where Nancy and I were born and grew up. She didn't know the churches that had nurtured us and prayed for us. She didn't recognize the grace gift God was giving us through her. He could have chosen any state. We would have gone. But he picked Missouri and prepared her people. We would be working with family. We were going home.

I wanted to say, "Let's call the state convention offices in Missouri and go to work." First, however, I knew I needed administrative approval from the person responsible for missions work in Lesotho, our area director, Davis Saunders. Beyond his approval, though, and vastly more important to me, I wanted Davis' support and involvement. I didn't just want a "go ahead." I wanted him to "catch the vision" and become a partner in this venture.

Davis was in Africa and would not be back in the Richmond office until the following day. Reluctantly, I asked Minette to keep our conversation confidential until I could brief Davis. I didn't want our director coming back into the office and hearing about plans that should have been discussed with him first. She understood the wisdom in my request and, with a corresponding reluctance, agreed to keep our conversation to herself.

Later, she told me, "You asked me to sit on this for the time being, and I found that I was so excited that I couldn't even sit in my chair." This kind of response was to be duplicated many times in the months ahead. People heard what God was doing in Missouri and Lesotho, and they couldn't sit still. An excitement, a desire to get involved, overtook them, and they could not remain neutral. They had to tell somebody. They had to join in.

Through the night and the next morning I prayed and rehearsed the conversation I would have with Davis. I decided not to try to sell him on this idea. Instead, I wanted only to testify of what God had done and shown. God would capture him. My approach was on track. My timing was off.

When I reached Davis the next morning, I asked about his trip and his schedule for the morning, "Do you have time to talk for a few minutes about something related to the Mission in Lesotho?"

He replied that he did, and so I began with a brief background and overview of the proposal. I knew that Davis would ask a number of questions, and we would discuss the fuller implications of the project.

Instead, he asked nothing. I wondered why. Then I heard a guilty chuckle on the other end of the line, and he confessed, "Randy, now I've got to tell you a story."

Minette had kept her word and not mentioned our talk with anyone at the Board. After leaving the office late that afternoon, she had dinner with her daughter who was visiting from out of town. Then they drove to the Richmond airport where her daughter caught a flight back to her home. After seeing her off, Minette was leaving the terminal when she spied longtime friend, Mary Saunders, sitting in one of the waiting areas. Mary, a former missionary nurse, is Davis' wife. Greeting Mary, Minette asked why she was at the airport. Mary responded that Davis' plane was due soon.

I knew what Davis was going to say next: Minette hadn't been able to keep the secret any longer. Soon, Mary knew all the details. When Davis stepped off the plane, he was met by two women bubbling over with a story he just had to hear. Now I understood why Davis hadn't asked me any questions. He had already prayed and thought through all the questions and their answers during the night. His decision had been made even before I had called. God had prepared him for this moment, and now God had captured him, too.

Not only did we have approval to contact Missouri Baptists and begin to explore the plan with them, Davis wanted this story to go even further. He asked me to come to Richmond in February. Foreign Mission Board members from across the country would be coming there for the Board's winter meeting. He wanted to give me his director's time before the full Board to share this story with them. From the beginning, the magnificent breadth of what God was doing and wanted to do through this plan for concerted prayer was overwhelming.

Davis and I finished talking. I called Minette back and we laughed together over what had transpired. Certainly, God had been in her meeting at the airport, but I teased her that I would have to think before I trusted her with another secret. Now it was time to move forward. I had another request of her. I knew some of the leaders in the Missouri Baptist Convention and could call them and begin discussions. I told her, though, that this potential linking of Missouri and Lesotho would be a Foreign Mission Board project and not a personal effort of the Sprinkles. Consequently, I felt that the first contact with the state should come not from us but from the Board directly. She agreed and offered to make the call. We talked about which state office should be contacted and decided that the Woman's Missionary Union was the logical first choice. Minette would call the director, Alberta Gilpin.

A few hours later our phone rang in Fort Worth, and a familiar voice greeted us. It was Alberta. Years before, we had furloughed in the Jefferson City area and met Alberta. When we realized that the three of us liked Chinese food, we started meeting regularly at a Chinese restaurant for lunch and fellowship. It had been a few years since we'd last been together, and as we talked I realized how much I missed those times.

Alberta told me of her conversation with Minette and started asking more details about the project. She was an experienced administrator. She already had seen that logistically a prayer network of this scope would be nearly impossible to plan and implement in the short time before spring and our departure for Lesotho. I knew this as well. I also knew that the entire next year, 1987, was planned and budgeted, and she and her staff had already begun work on the following year. A major project like this logically should have two years of lead time built into it. Yet what I had seen in Davis Saunders earlier I now saw in Alberta. To undertake this project on short notice would mean extensive reworking of plans and commitments as well as reallocation of budget funds. If this was what God desired, though, that settled it. Alberta would do whatever was necessary to follow His will. I came away from our conversation knowing that Alberta was open to the idea and guardedly excited about its rightness and potential.

Alberta explained that two planning meetings were scheduled over the next few days. The first was a WMU staff retreat focusing on praying and planning for future Missouri WMU missions work. The second meeting allowed the state WMU prayer coordinator to evaluate the current prayer efforts and discuss possible changes. These two meetings seemed to be quite a coincidence. As always, for what God purposes, He makes preparation. Alberta and I agreed to pray in the intervening days for God's will to be made more clear through the leaders in these meetings. She would present my proposal to the women, solicit their impressions, and call me again.

The news she brought to us the next week was thrilling. The women's initial reaction to such an undertaking was, "This is tremendous, but how can we actually do something like this?"

Both groups had heard Alberta's report and discussed its pros and cons. The results from both meetings were the same: "The idea has merit; implementing it seems unfeasible at this time; but there is something about this that we can't get away from."

The "something" was, of course, "Someone." The irrefutable stamp of God was upon the proposal. They saw this as we had, as Minette and Davis had, and as would the first dozens and eventually the thousands who would become troops in the intercessory trenches. The leaders agreed that they must pursue it another step. We would be in Missouri the next month to celebrate Christmas with our families.

Alberta asked, "While you're here, could you come to Jefferson City and meet with a group of WMU leaders?"

Excitedly, we said, "Yes." The meeting was set for December 22, 1986.

A cold blowing snow engulfed us as we left the children with my parents in Sullivan, Missouri, to begin the one-and-one-half-hour drive to Jefferson City. In homes around the state, women broke the busy flow of their Christmas preparations to reconsider their plans for the day. Should they drive to this hastily called meeting in threatening weather like this? When we arrived at the Baptist building in Jefferson City for the 10:00 A.M. meeting, their answers were obvious. Every single one was there. These women, with their vision for and commitment to missions, were representative of the group of people who would eventually be gathered from the entire state. This great group of intercessors would push on through many future storms, both physical and spiritual, simply because they had the conviction their task was from God. Included in the group Alberta had assembled were Norma Altis, the state WMU president; Marilyn Coble, the state WMU prayer coordinator; and Debbie Miller and Kathy Stahr, WMU associates for Missouri.

We planned to meet for two hours during which the group would hear our testimonies of how God had brought us to this decisive day. Discussion would follow and then a decision would be made. What we presented to these leaders was a proposal for something that had never been done before in Southern Baptist life. A state convention would link itself with a new Mission at its very beginning in an open-ended prayer partnership. Christians would be offered the opportunity to get under the burdens of Lesotho and her people and bear them up to God in prayer. As a result, God would have open to Him thousands of lives, channels through which He could pour out His gracious power and love. The recipient would be this little nation, unknown to most of the world, but precious to

God and, because of receptive, obedient lives, increasingly precious to Missouri Baptists.

Alberta made the introductions and we prayed. As I
began to talk about how this country opened, how the
prayer partnership idea had come about, and especially
how we were led to Missouri, I kept in mind our central
objective. My goal was to show God's initiating and guid-
ing role at each step, including the meeting in which we
now sat. I had utter confidence that if this were accomplished, the outcome was not in question.

The response of the participants told me that my goal
had been met. The immediate and unanimous consensus
was that surely God was the author of this. Their decision
to accept the proposal came early and fairly easily. As I listened to their discussions, I heard again a key phrase that
I had heard in my initial talk with Minette. Repeatedly, they
spoke of having "caught the vision." God was doing something new. He had chosen them. They weren't considering
a proposal from the Sprinkles or even from the Foreign
Mission Board. God had made clear His desire. When the
leaders reached this point in their deliberations, they realized their decision was already made for them. It was
inconceivable to respond in any other way than, "Yes."

At 12:20 that afternoon, all of us realized we were in the
midst of something we could not leave. We adjourned to a
local restaurant and continued the meeting. By 1:30 we
were back in the conference room where we worked until
4:00. Rather than spending all of the time wrestling with
whether to enter into this commitment, the bulk of the
day's work was spent developing the structure and plans
for the Missouri/Lesotho Prayer Partnership.

Alberta and her staff would rework the plans and budget to give priority to the partnership. It was decided,
though, that two more steps would be essential in the
catch-the-vision process that was at work. First, associational WMU prayer coordinators and other leaders must
hear firsthand about the partnership and its background.
Second, the largest possible group of people from the
churches of the state also must hear the story for themselves. The group acknowledged the importance of as
many people as possible having a personal encounter

with God and His call to them. Each person needed to hear an individual call and then make the commitment before God to accept this responsibility.

A schedule was prepared. In February 1987 I would travel to Richmond, Virginia, to meet with the Foreign Mission Board and share with them what God was doing through prayer in Missouri and Lesotho. In March, Alberta would organize a series of meetings in five different regions of Missouri. Associational leaders would be informed of these meetings and their purpose, and she and I, along with the state WMU president and prayer coordinator, would tour the state carrying the message. Finally, in April, I would speak to the annual meeting of the Missouri WMU. Here I would have the opportunity to address 1,200 to 1,500 women from every part of the state. Immediately after the annual meeting, Nancy and I and the boys would leave for Lesotho to begin the work of establishing the Mission.

As we drove away from Jefferson City that evening, we encountered a thick winter fog. The trip back to my parents' home was slow and difficult. This day, when we had seen so much of the future materialize before us, was now ending strangely as we could barely see beyond the front of the car. We didn't know it, but we were witnessing a prototype, a pattern, for our work ahead. Rarely would we see very far ahead in Lesotho. This was not a walk of sight we were entering. It was a walk of faith, as rightly it should be. And like the trip home that night, each bit of progress in Lesotho was going to be slow and difficult.

But in April 1987, as we were making final preparations to leave Southwestern Seminary and travel, via Missouri, to Lesotho, the future looked to be quite the opposite. The December meeting had been successful beyond our dreams. The February trip to Richmond and the Foreign Mission Board had been a blessed experience. Seeds for future prayer endeavors were planted that day in trustees from across the country as they heard God's call to prayer in Missouri. Every stop of the March trip around the state was met with women and men who were open, receptive, and, by the time we left, committed to their intercessory place in the Lesotho Baptist Mission. We had decided upon a name for the partnership: Lift Up Lesotho. That title would fly as a banner over all that the partnership would engage in through the years ahead. It spoke of what we were about.

Alberta was in her office. Nancy and I were in our car on the road to Missouri. Each of us was moving toward the WMU annual meeting to be held in a few days. From different perspectives we were reflecting upon the amazing events of these past few months. There had been a host of surprises in 1987 after all—pleasant surprises— each one more blessed than the one before. Now this annual meeting was to be the culmination. In power we were praying. The forces would be marshaled. The advance would begin.

We couldn't know that the Enemy also had some surprises for this year—painful, costly surprises.

5

A Birth Announcement

The days were going to be bittersweet for us: bitter because we were leaving home, sweet because we were going back home. They would also be painful because they were "good-bye" days; and from experience, we knew what they could be like. In just two weeks, on April 15, we would be leaving for Africa again.

For the moment, we weren't thinking of that day. No one even spoke of it. We were visiting my parents before WMU annual meeting. After that, we would travel to Nancy's home for a few days before flying out of St. Louis. The scene that warm spring afternoon offered a typical slice of American life. Three generations of a family—a grandfather, a father, and a grandson—were contentedly sitting around a backyard picnic table. We were enjoying a few moments together, rare moments because two-thirds of our trio lived most of our lives far away from this home and its familiar surroundings. We were happy. A closer look, though, would have shown the happiness to be tainted by the approaching separation.

Inside the house, Nancy and my mother were talking in muted tones. Stephen, 15 months old, was sleeping in an adjoining bedroom. He was uncomfortable because of a cold, and we were not looking forward to a long transatlantic flight with a fussy baby. For now, like most parents, we were content to relish the quiet that naptime brings.

A painting of this moment would have shown a tranquil scene of a family at home. It would have been wrong. Even a Norman Rockwell eye for subtle detail would have missed a key element of the setting, for there was also danger in that day. The danger was beyond the physical world at this moment, but it was about to move into the physical world. We knew to be alert. We knew our Enemy prowled about, unseen, nearby. We didn't see, though, that in that small Missouri town an ambush had been set—and the first moment of attack had arrived. The idyllic setting was about to disintegrate into confusion and fear. The cue for the scene change was to be a scream.

Inside, Nancy had gone to another part of the house when a brief, faint cry came from the bedroom. Normally, since Stephen had been asleep only a short time, we would have waited to go in, hoping he would go back to sleep. Grandmothers, though, operate according to a different set of guidelines. As much as parents enjoy the quiet of naptimes, grandmothers find any excuse to hold their grandbabies. This little cry was all Grandmother needed. Now she could legitimately go get the baby even if he should have been left to sleep another hour. As Mother carried Stephen from the bedroom, he stopped breathing.

Outside on the patio, we heard not his whimper, only her scream.

Those next minutes were ones of pandemonium. I ran into the house. Stephen was stiff. He was already changing color as I took him from my mother. *Is he choking?* I asked myself. *What's causing this?* I thought as I ran my hands and my eyes over him, trying to find some hint of the trouble. Somehow, I already had him lying on the floor.

"He's hot. He's way too hot. And he's not breathing," I said. I started stripping off his clothes as I shouted, "Get a cold wet towel!"

Nancy was crying and praying. I was working on Stephen on the floor, trying to get air into his lungs, trying to help him breathe again. Grandma was frantically calling an ambulance—and then calling again when it didn't arrive instantly.

44

Finally, we could hear the siren. It seemed to take forever for the ambulance to arrive. Then the paramedics were in the house assessing Stephen, moving him to the ambulance. As we rode in the back of the swaying vehicle to the Sullivan Hospital, Stephen took irregular, short breaths. He was alive, but something was terribly wrong.

The hours in the emergency room were traumatic for all of us. Stephen cried most of the time. We waited and prayed, our minds swirling with the possibilities: What's wrong with him? He's alive, but has his brain already been damaged? What is this going to mean for him and for all of us? Finally, the doctor told us that he wanted to call for a medical evacuation helicopter from Barnes Hospital in St. Louis. Stephen needed to be taken there as quickly as possible. Hesitantly, we asked what he thought was wrong. His answer was like a nightmare, "We suspect he may have contracted spinal meningitis."

Our shock seemed to shorten the time it took for the helicopter to arrive. On board were a pediatric doctor and nurse. They worked quickly to ready Stephen for the trip; and then the helicopter took off and we were alone in the darkness. As we walked to the car, Nancy asked, "Did you see the round button the medevac nurse had pinned to her uniform?"

I thought for a moment as I unlocked the car. "No, I didn't notice it."

"It said, 'Real life really isn't like this.'"

As we packed a few things at my parents' house and loaded the car for the drive to St. Louis, we had to say, "Real life shouldn't be like this, but sometimes it is."

Before we left, I gave my mother the name and telephone number of the state WMU prayer coordinator and asked that she call her. Not until after 10:00 that Saturday night did Mother reach Marilyn Coble. Far later into the night, Marilyn put her own telephone down for the last time. All over Missouri lights were coming on and sleepy minds were struggling to comprehend what they were hearing. It was more than a report. It was a call for reinforcements. Without driving to St. Louis, these warriors immediately came to our aid. Although they didn't hear the cry or even the scream, the call to prayer was enough. We weren't alone in the darkness any longer. They had joined us and they had joined God—for the battle was His.

We endured the long night in the hospital, meeting with doctors and authorizing tests. Slowly a new day, Sunday, came as we peered wearily through the glass wall of Stephen's isolation room. Waiting for the test results, we knew that God was not absent. Not only was He providing for our family, He had provided for us in preparation for this hour.

At some point during that long night and the following day, we thought of our tenuous finances and the bills we were incurring. By deciding to stay at seminary until I finished my graduate work, we had exhausted our furlough time and gone on a leave of absence. During leave, we received neither furlough salary nor medical insurance through the Foreign Mission Board. To compensate for the insurance loss, we had purchased medical insurance through the seminary plan, but our financial situation had become increasingly more difficult. There in the hospital, Nancy and I remembered the decision we had faced just a few weeks before.

Our medical insurance bill of $155 had come for the month of April. What should we do? On April 15 we would return to active missionary service so we would have Foreign Mission Board medical insurance again. If we didn't pay this bill, however, there would be a two-week period from April 1-14 when we would have no insurance at all. Should we take this risk? We took the decision to God for His perfect guidance. Then we paid the premium. On April 4, 1987, Stephen was stricken, and his medical bills eventually exceeded $7,000. They were covered.

Sitting together in the hospital, we acknowledged this powerful reminder of God's foreknowing care for us. Our faith in Him and in His care for Stephen was bolstered and brightened. We could trust Him with renewed confidence. We also did not view as coincidence the timing of this episode. Because it was Sunday, intercessors all over the state were going to their churches. There they were spreading word of our need. In Sunday Schools and morning worship services, entire Baptist congregations were joining together in prayer for Stephen.

By Sunday afternoon, a doctor met with us. In his hand was the test result for spinal meningitis. It was negative!

We had seen in the space of less than 24 hours a snapshot of how God plans for His children to work with Him in the advance of His kingdom on earth. A year earlier I had researched the history of a number of spiritual awakenings. The pattern I found in all of them was this: The path that led to awakening and to the great struggles and resistance that always accompanied it began with God and moved to a solitary figure bowed in prayer. Later, others who were prepared, sensitive, and willing would join the work of prayer until finally a whole legion of pray-ers were laboring together with God and the victory was achieved.

In just a few days, the Lord of Hosts was going to issue the call to a host of Missouri Baptists to enter this Lesotho battle and see it through to victory. The Enemy, at all costs, needed to thwart this. Satan knows that work without prayer is work without power, and from that he has nothing to fear. So while Satan will harass and disturb us as we go about our work, his chief concern is to hinder prayer—he nearly had. He knew that if the prayer partnership came into being, God would have a mighty channel and facility for His power to come to earth, not only in Lesotho but in Missouri as well. Satan saw what the result of this would be. The Holy Spirit would come in increasing power on Lesotho. The nation would be blessed. People would be liberated. Satan would be routed.

The most promising way to stop all of this before it could even begin was a preemptive strike. Where should the attack come? Strike the missionary family. Take them out of the picture at the last moment. This would confuse and demoralize the intercessors. The prayer partnership would unravel and the great danger would pass.

This was not a surprise to God because He had permitted it. The first two chapters of the book of Job make clear that while God loves and cares for His children, He also, at times, allows Satan to bring pain and distress upon us. It seems, in the midst of this, that God is absent. He is not.

During these times, God also provides for Himself a way back into our situation. For us, it had come during the previous month. Through our trip around Missouri, He had called into position a small group of intercessors: the associational WMU directors and prayer coordinators. They thought their real work would begin when we left for Lesotho. Instead, an emergency call came early and they had been ready and responsive.

We rejoiced that Stephen did not have spinal meningitis. However, since we were taking Stephen to a place where medical care was limited, we wanted to understand clearly what had happened to him. The next days in the hospital were puzzling. The doctors were unable to find anything wrong with Stephen except a cold. Finally, they could only speculate that a virus or a small sinus infection had caused a sudden high fever to short-circuit the electrical impulses in his body and interrupt his breathing. The terrors of the week were past; Stephen was fine.

On Thursday, April 9, the eve of the WMU annual meeting, we took Stephen from the hospital to Nancy's parents' home in St. Louis. We were relieved and grateful. We were also exhausted.

Instead of leaving the next morning for Jefferson City and the annual meeting with high anticipation and bright hopes as we planned, I drove out of St. Louis alone. My mood was somber and reflective as I left a wounded and hurting family that needed me. The two-and-a-half-hour trip became more than just a physical journey into another part of the state. My soul journeyed into a deeper, disturbing understanding of what I was facing and what would be asked of my family. Motorists who passed me thought I was traveling alone. During heavy periods of our lives, it does often seem to others, and even to us, that we walk alone. I had a traveling companion, though. He was unseen and He was undaunted by what had transpired or by what was yet to come. The time on the road was one of prayer, of communion with God, the God.

We had not drawn easy assignments before in our mission service. We understood about struggle and perseverance and difficulty. I came to recognize, however, in those hours on the highway that we did not understand the level or intensity of struggle, spiritual and physical, that lay ahead. This last week had been a sample, a foretaste. A great deal more was to come. The establishing of this new Mission was going to be costly. We, our future missionary colleagues, and the intercessors of Missouri were being called to pay the price.

I needed this insight, though it was not attractive and not an encouragement, to stay the course. On the contrary, my strong temptation was to look for a way out—to think, forget it; to say maybe we'd better reconsider this. Whether those thoughts came from my own mind or were whispered into my consciousness by the Father of Lies, to this day I'm not sure. I do know they were given consideration—and rejected.

Driving into Jefferson City that April day, I also understood that the pain and trauma of these recent days had a purpose far beyond simple personal attack. Satan's ultimate intention had been exposed: the Missouri/Lesotho Prayer Partnership must not be born!

Later that day I left my motel room and began the walk to the First Baptist Church and the two days of meetings. I was neither excited nor distressed. I felt no special power or inspiration. As I arrived at the church and saw the crowds of women registering and filling the sanctuary, I was simply determined, convicted: Labor is about to begin and by tomorrow the Missouri/Lesotho Prayer Partnership is going to be birthed.

I took the pulpit that afternoon for the first of my two general session assignments. I stood before a group of women who were informed and expectant. They were ready, in part, because Alberta and her staff had done the necessary work to prepare them. In early March, Alberta had asked us to write a personal letter to all of the associational WMU prayer coordinators. In it, we introduced ourselves and gave a brief background of the Lesotho Mission and our leadership to Missouri. The letter included a small picture of our family and the first Lift Up Lesotho monthly prayer guide, dated April 1987. Alberta also had revised the printed program for the annual meeting to include a full page of information on Lesotho and the prayer partnership. Finally, she had arranged for the state Baptist paper, *Word and Way*, to print an extensive article on March 5, 1987, giving a background on us, the opening of Lesotho, and the plans for the prayer partnership.

Those women, numbering over 1,000 who sat before me were not only informed, they were honed to a keen spiritual edge. The experiences of the last days had provided a piece of preparation that human plans could never have. These women had come alongside of us. The feelings of helplessness and dependence that we felt, they also had experienced. The struggle of faith and prayer that was ours had become theirs as well. Through the past week, a bond had been formed with us and with a little mountain country named Lesotho. In those dark days, God had taken the final step in readying these people for this high hour.

The stage was gloriously set, and I was determined not to take it!

This was not a setting where I would preach my heart out. Instead, I wanted it to be a time when I opened my heart and let these friends look inside. As they looked through this window, I wanted them to see God's desire for them and for the Basotho people.

On Friday afternoon, I walked them through our missionary years, some of our key molding experiences, and our leading to this climactic annual meeting. In the Saturday morning session, we met God and heard His call to prayer and His call to Lesotho.

Then the time came for decision. Before them, in my hand, I raised a leather-bound book. Its first two pages held handwritten words, the rest were blank. I began to read to them from the book. I read a covenant, a prayer covenant, not with us, but between them and God.

I asked the women to consider this call upon their lives with its costs and then to respond. I told them that I was taking the book and going into the building next door which housed the missionary mall. There, at the Lesotho booth, I would wait for them through the middle hours of the day until the beginning of the closing session that afternoon. When each of them had come to a decision, they could search me out and sign their names in the book to this covenant:

Lift Up Lesotho Prayer Covenant

"Ask, and it shall be given to you; seek, and you shall find; knock, and it shall be opened to you" (Matt. 7:7 NASB).

By the grace of God and to His glory, we joyfully enter into a covenant of intercessory prayer for God's spiritual blessings in the African nation of Lesotho. In so doing, we give priority in our own lives to prayer and to gathering others together to pray to this end.

As we go to God in prayer, we will seek to come to Him prepared, in heart and mind, to intercede without hindrance according to His desires.

We will be alert to His responses as we pray that our intercessions may always be guided by the progressive unfolding of His will in Lesotho and in our lives.

By His grace, we will persist in prayer until spiritual awakening is brought to reality in Lesotho.

Recognizing that awakening is born in and sustained by a movement of prayer, we will not only intercede personally, but we will also be faithful to call upon God to raise up others to join with us in prayer.

I walked to the adjoining building and took my place at the Lesotho booth, wondering what kind of response these women would make. I did not have to wonder long. As soon as the session was adjourned, women began to flow into the mall and look for me. Almost immediately there were too many to get to the book and a line began to form. The wait was protracted. Many of the women chose to skip lunch rather than relinquish their opportunity to make this commitment. For the next two hours, there was an unspoken, visual testimony of these Missouri Baptists' convictions as they waited their turn to sign the covenant and formalize their surrender to God's call.

That afternoon I slipped into the rear foyer of the church for the closing session of the meeting. I carried in my hand a book with page after page filled with hundreds of names of newly committed intercessors. The Missouri/Lesotho Prayer Partnership had been born!

Just as I was about to enter the church sanctuary, a woman stopped me. At first, she seemed to be at a loss for words. Then, with a smile she shook her finger at me and declared, "Do you know this is the first time in my life I ever had to wait in line to pray for somebody."

6

No Vacancy

"I'm sorry, Mr. Sprinkle, but we have no reservations in your name, and the flight is full."

The day had already been a long one, and it was still early afternoon. As I left the ticket counter at Kennedy Airport in New York and walked back to my waiting family, I feared it was going to get much longer.

The day had begun in the predawn darkness as my brother-in-law, John Allen, had helped me load five footlockers into his van and transport them to Lambert International Airport in St. Louis. Since it would be several months before we received our crate of household goods in Lesotho, the few carefully selected items in these footlockers would comprise our initial household "outfit." This was all we would have to set up our household with until our crate arrived. At the airport, I checked the footlockers as excess baggage on the flight we would board later in the morning. Then we returned to my mother-in-law's home for breakfast, the loading of suitcases, and those dreaded good-byes.

The days leading up to this morning culminated in the most difficult departure we had ever experienced. This was particularly true for Nancy. For the first time ever, she was experiencing extreme difficulty in preparing herself mentally for the new culture and challenges we would face. Adding to her turmoil were the advanced age and

53

declining health of her father. She sensed she was waving good-bye to him that morning for the last time on this earth. Sadly, she was correct.

Adding to the struggle, Stephen had been stricken, and the last days and nights had blurred together in a haze of apprehension and exhaustion. As our departure date approached, we had our things together, but we didn't have ourselves together. We needed time to rest, but we also needed to get to Lesotho and begin to reestablish the stable base of a home. Finally, we compromised and delayed our departure one week to April 22.

The extra days in the spring of 1987 proved to be of little help to us. On Tuesday Nancy admitted, "Only one thing will get me on that plane tomorrow: obedience to God. I'm not ready and I don't want to go."

Then, another minor crisis had developed. Matthew, our nine-year-old, had lost his teddy bear. "Ted T" was the handmade creation of Matthew's grandmother and the one friend who didn't have to be left behind every time we traveled to a new place. Now he was gone. We searched every possible hiding place in Grandma's house, but on the last morning, Ted T was still missing. We assured Matthew that when we closed the suitcases and straightened the rooms, Ted T would turn up. He didn't.

As I carried our bags out and loaded them, I felt that this lost family friend might be our proverbial last straw.

The front door stood open. The family gathered. Everyone fought back tears. Hugs and kisses were passed all around. At last, we started out the door when, without warning, Matthew turned and ran back into the house.

Oh no, I thought, *this is it. He's going to refuse to leave.*

"Come on, Son," I implored gently. "It's time to go. We've got to leave or we will miss our plane."

We saw Matthew run into the dining room and over to the china cabinet. We stood transfixed as he opened the glass door, reached back into a corner, and through the dishes and glasses somehow extracted Ted T.

Earlier in the week the teddy bear had found the perfect hiding place. It was only at this last instant that Matthew remembered where he was hiding.

Suddenly, the whole mood of the moment changed. The tension broke. Everyone laughed. Matthew wore a radiant smile that got us out of the house and onto a jet heading toward New York and the other flights that would take us again to Africa.

Cruising high above the clouds on our way to New York, I wanted to believe the worst must be behind us. I thanked God for the little gifts of grace that meant so much. I also thanked Him for that band of intercessors back in Missouri who each minute were farther and farther behind us and yet through prayer were also out ahead of us. They were running interference for us, smoothing the way. I laid my head back and rested. We could count on our intercessors and we could count on God. Surely now things would begin to get better.

And then I encountered the reservation agent in New York City.

"What's wrong?" Apparently the look on my face telegraphed our situation before I even reached Nancy.

"Honey, we definitely have confirmed tickets for the flight, but somehow the airline doesn't have our reservation," I answered.

The look on Nancy's face as she slowly pushed Stephen back and forth in the portable stroller began to reflect the same concern that I was feeling.

"Can't they just go ahead and book us on the flight now?"

"I'm afraid not. The flight is full, and, to make matters worse, they have overbooked it by 50 passengers."

"What are we going to do?"

Both of us knew that the flight we were planning to take was scheduled only once a week. We couldn't lay over in New York for seven days. The few other international flights would not easily connect us with the airlines on which we held tickets in Europe and eastern Africa. Missing those connections would result in missing other connections on to southern Africa. We needed to get on this flight.

"You start praying and I'll go back to the counter."

Through our years of traveling and a few close calls, Nancy and I had developed a personal rule regarding New

York. We would never fly through this city without at least four hours between flights. I was thankful, as I walked back to the airline representative, that we had stayed with our rule in making the flight schedule for this trip. We still had over three hours to work on the problem.

Since it was early, no one else was at the counter as I began to talk to the airline representative about our situation. Pointing to the confirmation code on our tickets, I reminded him that our travel agent could not have issued the tickets without the approval of his airline. I also gave him the name of the travel agency in Baltimore that had handled our reservations. He was surprised when I also produced the telephone number of the agency and the name of the agent who had handled our arrangements. I asked him to call the agent and sort out the problem.

Over the next half hour, I watched as the airline representative made calls and consulted with his supervisor. I passed our tickets to him when he asked for them and later handed over our passports as well. When finally he returned with all our papers, I saw that on the top were four boarding passes with seat assignments.

"Have a nice flight, Mr. Sprinkle. Sorry for the delay."

I didn't ask how he had resolved the situation. I just thanked him; and then as I headed across the waiting area toward my family, I thanked God.

Nancy didn't have to read my expression this time. With a thumbs-up, I fairly shouted, "We're on!"

The change in aircraft altitude signaled a descent. Peering eagerly out the window, I began to recognize the familiar sights of Jan Smuts Airport in Johannesburg, South Africa. Our two days of flying from New York through Amsterdam and Nairobi were finally over. We were back.

Coming out of Customs and Immigration we spied an old friend from Ethiopian days, Cliff Staton. After the breakup of the Ethiopian Mission in the late seventies, Cliff and his wife, Philecta, had followed the twists and turns of God's will to Mission assignments here in South Africa. We were delighted to be met by this friend. Cliff helped us load pushcarts with our bags and the five footlockers that we had checked in St. Louis two-and-one-half days before. Not a single piece of our luggage was missing.

We emerged into the familiar hot African sun and began to follow Cliff. We walked and walked and walked.

"Where are you parked, Cliff?" I panted.

"You'll see. It's right over there," he answered smiling.

Cliff was pointing to a new four-wheel drive, double-cab pickup. Our urban missionaries didn't use this type of vehicle, so I suspected whose this one might be.

Sure enough, Cliff grinned, "I thought you might like to ride in your new Lesotho Mission vehicle." It was the exact vehicle I had requested months earlier.

After filling the back of the truck with our luggage, we climbed into the cab and headed for the Baptist guest house. A wave of gratitude swept over us—gratitude to God, to the Foreign Mission Board, and especially to the people of the churches who had made the purchase of this new truck possible through Lottie Moon Christmas Offering gifts. We drove into the parking lot of the guest house and there were met with another surprise. Pete and Becky Baer, our colleagues during our years in the Kalahari, were in Johannesburg on business and had waited over to welcome us back. In spite of our fatigue, we felt welcomed and excited. This day was the first really bright one for us in quite a while.

We had determined our first two goals must be acquiring a temporary visa to Lesotho and finding a place to live, so the day after our arrival I placed a call to Maseru, the capital city of Lesotho. In Botswana in 1980, we had become friends with a Mission Aviation Fellowship (MAF) couple, Steve and Judy Holz. After leaving Botswana they had served in other countries in southern Africa before eventually being sent to Lesotho. I had written them as soon as we knew we would be coming and asked them to be on the alert for housing. I had told them I would call them when we arrived in Johannesburg. As I talked to Steve, I learned that housing was difficult to find, but he had located a couple of small bungalows that were marginal but available. I told him we would take one just to get a place to live and then look for something better later. He also told me that they had experienced no problems in obtaining multimonth visas through the immigration office. We made plans to enter Lesotho the next Friday, May 1.

Hanging up the phone, I began to feel more assured that the difficulties of the past months were behind us. The prayers of the Missouri intercessors finally were bearing fruit. After all, hadn't God promised to meet our needs? Sharing the good news from the Holzes, however, I realized Nancy wasn't convinced that we had turned the corner. She remained in turmoil about what lay ahead.

I tried to reassure her while at the same time redoubling my own efforts in prayer. I asked and expected God to speak words of encouragement and reassurance to her. Instead, I began to sense that all would not be as smooth as it seemed. I became increasingly uneasy about what I thought I was understanding. I struggled with knowing whether it was God Who was warning me or the Enemy who was trying to discourage. On the eve of our leaving Johannesburg, God clarified for me that it was He Who was speaking, and I was not misunderstanding Him.

That night as I read from my Bible and prayed, the Holy Spirit highlighted two verses of Scripture for me. In Joshua 1:9, I read, "Be strong and courageous! Do not tremble or be dismayed, for the Lord your God is with you wherever you go" (NASB). I received this word as one of both exhortation and strong assurance. I also knew at that moment that Lesotho and our work there were going to be more difficult than we could imagine—even fearsome.

The other word which was given by God to us that evening was from John 15:7: "If you abide in Me, and My words abide in you, ask whatever you wish, and it shall be done for you" (NASB). No matter what lay ahead, God desired our ongoing trust. We were to keep an unbroken connection to Him. This word from the Lord told me much about the nature of what awaited us. We were to face trials that would threaten our very communion with God and thus our channel for receiving His sustaining grace.

Rolling south out of Johannesburg the next morning, I reflected on the contrasts between this trip and that one years ago when we had first seen the mountains of Lesotho. That day we were only passing by. Today we were entering in. That day the future was distant and indistinct. Today it was clear and at hand. That day we were animated and excited. Today we were quiet and resolute.

In the early afternoon, we cleared the South African border post. We pulled onto the rusty single-lane bridge spanning the Caledon River and saw Lesotho just ahead. Crossing slowly, I glanced at the muddy swirling waters below. They mirrored the currents that flowed along the borders of our own lives this day.

Then we were across. There were no cameras or news teams to record the moment. The intercessors back in Missouri could not see this and feel the rush. They could only imagine this first small victory of their Mission and give thanks to God.

Not only was there no one to record the event, there was no time to enjoy it. Directly ahead of us stood a fence, a closed gate, and a group of border guards. Our first test had come. At the border office we would request a temporary visitor's visa that would allow us sufficient time to secure our permanent resident visa from the immigration office in Maseru. We entered the building and began completing the immigration forms. The official who waited on us was sullen and unresponsive. We requested a 90-day visa. The official offered two weeks. I explained to her why we were entering Lesotho and why we needed more time. She showed no indication of having heard me and began stamping our passports. In a moment, she pushed our visas across the counter to us and turned away. As we walked outside to the truck, I opened my passport and looked at the visa. We had 30 days.

In my rearview mirror, I saw the border gate close behind us. In front of us was a new world that we expected to be our home for the rest of our missions years. As I shifted through the truck's gears, I thought, *We've only got 30 days to secure this future, or we're out of this country before we hardly begin.* Following the directions Steve had given me to his home, I thanked God that at least we had a place to live.

A warm welcome awaited us at the Holzes' house. The new baby we had known in Botswana was a pretty little school girl now and the young boy in the house was her brother we had heard about but never met. Visiting these old friends, we felt ties and a sense of belonging. It was nice to know someone in Lesotho. The small amount of security that seeing our friends brought, however, quickly dissipated when Steve broke the bad news to us.

Earlier they had gone to get the key to the little house we were going to rent. When they arrived, they learned the manager had rented both houses to someone else. Steve and Judy had called several places to see if they could locate something else for us before we arrived, but nothing was available. Thirty days might be *more* time than we needed after all, if we couldn't find a place to live.

The shortage of housing in Maseru was the consequence of the initiation of a 20- to 30-year development program called the Highlands Water Project. The international effort was going to result in the building of several dams in the massive canyons. The water in the lakes that were to be built would be diverted through generators and then into pipelines for sale to energy- and water-hungry South Africa. It would be the all-time biggest boost to the Lesotho economy. The project had just gotten started, and employees of the companies had rented all of the available housing in the weeks just before our arrival.

The Holzes offered to let us stay at their house, but we did not want to impose on them. We asked about other options where we might temporarily rent even a room. Steve mentioned that an older hotel in town, the Victoria, might have something. We drove there and met the manager. He was a Scottish man and very sympathetic to our problem. "I'm sorry," he said, "the hotel is completely full, and I don't know when I might have a vacancy."

I heard what he said, but I knew that in Africa no doesn't always mean exactly that. I tried again. "I'm aware of the situation here in Maseru, but we are desperate for someplace to live. Are you sure you don't have something somewhere that we could rent?"

His hesitation in answering told me that he indeed was holding something back. I waited him out, and finally he said, "Well, you know I do have one room." Then quickly he added, "But I know you wouldn't be interested in it."

"I might be. Could we take a look at it?"

He excused himself for a moment and went to get a key. I glanced across at Steve and our eyes met. This was getting interesting.

Leading us to an adjacent building, he opened the door to the end room. It was small and not very clean, but it had two beds, a bathroom, and a small kitchenette. It was not what we were looking for, and it was too small for a family of four, but it was a start. The exorbitant rent did not surprise me in the current market. What did surprise me was that it was even available. I was suspicious.

Looking the manager in the eyes, I asked, "Why is this room not rented?"

For a moment he was taken aback, then he headed for the door, motioning for me to follow. Outside I found him standing by the corner of the building. He pointed to a sidewalk that ran along the outside wall of the room. It led to a door. Gesturing toward it, he said, "That's the hotel's disco bar." He paused, then continued. "It plays music every night." He waited another moment. "It plays *loud* music every night."

I was beginning to get the picture. "When is this disco open?"

"It's open every night," another pause, "from 10:00 P.M. until 6:00 A.M. the next morning."

I groaned. Now I understood why the room was vacant.

Looking at me, he said, "I've rented this room several times, but no one's ever been able to last in it for more than two or three days."

With no other options to consider and believing we could bear just about anything for a while, I rented the room for three days.

I knew, as I began looking around the city the next day, that somewhere God must have a house or apartment for us. I also knew that our intercessors were praying for housing and would not cease until we sent them word that it had been provided. On the third day, I walked back to the manager's office. Not only had I found nothing to rent, but I had not even been able to locate any promising leads. I paid the rent on our room for the rest of May. Two more times I would make this trip. The room that we thought might be our home for three days was to be the first residence of the Baptist Mission of Lesotho for three months.

Eventually, I followed up more than 100 leads without

success. Every night the music blasted, and Stephen would follow what became his regular pattern. Over and over through the night, he would fall asleep and then wake up crying. Of course, the rest of the family could not sleep either. The stress and fatigue mounted over the weeks. Added to this difficulty was the danger of the area. Repeatedly, we had shootings and stranglings just outside our window. Fights were nightly occurrences. Each evening we would barricade ourselves inside the room. In the morning we would unblock and open the door and clear away the broken beer bottles and vomit.

Across the Caledon River on the South African side of the border was the lovely farming town of Ladybrand. One day we traveled over there to take Stephen to the doctor and saw a house for rent. I asked about it, and before the day was over, I learned there were houses of various sizes available all over the town.

Instead of this being a breakthrough, it meant further distress. We were determined to do nothing that would adversely affect the future and reputation of Baptists and the Mission in Lesotho. Our personal situation could be easily resolved by packing up and moving to a nice house across the river. Then I could just drive back to Maseru to work, continuing to look for housing. But what would this say to the Basotho about us and about Baptists? By moving across the river, we would be moving to South Africa. The Basotho might view this as having racist overtones, and this could echo down through the years hindering the ministries of the other missionaries who would come to join us. No, we would stay in the "disco flat."

A few weeks after word reached Missouri of our housing difficulties, letters began to arrive. The Missouri intercessors were intensifying their prayer efforts while encouraging us to hang in there. One day we received a letter from a pray-er with an obvious sense of humor. It was addressed to the Disco Mission.

While our housing problems persisted, our 30-day visa was ticking down. My inquiries at the Immigration Office regarding the resident visa, for which we had applied months before, brought this response: "I'm sorry, Rev. Sprinkle, but your papers seem to have gone missing."

Anticipating that something like this might happen, I had written down every bit of information from our applications that I could—application numbers, dates, form numbers. I gave these to the clerk.

The clerk said she would look for our papers and told me I could come back next week.

We spent the next days in more house hunting and continual prayer for our visa. The end of May was nearing, and we would have to leave the country if we didn't get a visa. After a week I returned to the immigration office. When the clerk saw me, she went to a file cabinet and came back carrying a file folder. My heart leaped. Could this be our visa? Had God already answered? Yes! Surely this must be it.

"Rev. Sprinkle, I have found your papers. Everything seems to be in order."

"Do you have our resident visa?" I asked hopefully.

"Oh no," she answered, "it's not yet ready."

My heart sank. We had only a few days left on our visitor's visa. "How much longer do you think it might take before you could have it for us?"

The clerk studied our forms and then answered slowly and deliberately, "Since everything appears to be in order, and if no problems develop, I think that you should have your resident visa in about three . . . "

I was hanging on her every word, and when she reached this point I thought, *Is she going to say three days, three weeks? How long? I don't think we could wait over in South Africa for three months.*

She continued, "years."

I was dumbstruck. Had I heard her correctly? "Did you say three *years*?" I asked.

"Yes, that is correct. Three years."

Walking back to the disco flat, I realized how serious our situation had become. We could travel back and forth from South Africa for a while, getting a new visitor's visa each time we reentered the country. This we could do for a few weeks or even two or three months—but three years! That was impossible. As I shared this latest piece of bad news with Nancy, a phrase from Genesis came to my mind: "Is anything too difficult for the Lord?"

Humanly speaking, our housing prospects were impossible and so was our visa situation. Our current living conditions were barely tolerable. Our strength, mentally and physically, was about gone. Only God could pour hope and deliverance into our lives at this point, and, yes, He was able.

We had to begin packing our things in preparation for going out of the country for a few days. Just before our visa expired, though, I went back to the immigration office one more time. The same lady came to speak to me. I showed her our passports. As I spoke, I remembered the intercessors and their covenant with God. "Ask and you shall receive."

"Our visa is expiring. We don't want to leave Lesotho. I'm asking you to give us another visitor's visa so we can stay longer."

Without answering, she picked up our passports and disappeared into the inner offices. During the minutes that I waited, I reminded God of His covenant promise to us. When she returned, she handed our passports to me. Could it be? This seemed too easy. I thanked her and resisted the temptation to open them right then to see if anything had been entered in them.

Once outside on Kingsway, the main street of the capital city, I stopped and opened my passport. There I found a new visa stamped. I checked the dates. It was for six months. I wanted to dance right there on Kingsway. But of course, I didn't. What would the Foreign Mission Board think if they found out that the disco mission had become the "dancing mission?"

The new visa gave us the breathing room we needed to work in more detail on getting our resident visa. In time, I learned the course that our application must follow. I learned which officials must sign it and in what sequence. When our papers were sent from one office to another, I followed a day or two later to ensure that they made the trip. I came to know the secretaries in each of the key offices, and they came to know me. I never left an official's office without asking when I could return to check on our visa. When they would not give me a day, I would say, "All right, I'll just stop in next Tuesday when I'm in this part of town." Our papers were never lost again and they were never far from the top of the stack on whichever desk they rested.

While our visa application progressed, our personal situation continued to deteriorate. Winter was arriving and it was already getting quite cold. Our room had little heat and Nancy was sick much of the time with various ailments that were apparently brought on by viruses common in Lesotho winters. She really needed to get plenty of rest and minimize her stress, but our everyday (and every night) life precluded this completely. These first months were very painful for her.

Stephen also seemed to be sick all of the time. Without sleep, he was continually tired and cranky and his resistance was low. Each time he got sick, we were anxious because of his episode just before we left the States.

We had been very thankful that a place was available in the Maseru International School for Matthew. The school was English medium (taught in English) and had students from over 40 countries, but culturally Matthew experienced great difficulty finding a place to fit in. We prayed and prayed for a friend for him, but he steadily became more unhappy and withdrawn. One day when Nancy and I were having our regular discussion about our increasingly desperate situation, Matthew said, "God called us to Lesotho, but while we were on our way here He must have changed His mind and forgot to tell us." We had to admit to him that our circumstances did look like that.

Crime was a constant danger to us as well, and we were always on the lookout. One afternoon I parked our truck in the main parking lot of the small city mall. I needed to walk up to the post office and then stop at a building to check about a housing possibility. After checking at the post office I started up the street. Suddenly, I was impressed that I should forget making the inquiry today and just go on back to the flat. I turned around and walked back to the parking lot. I didn't sense anything was wrong until I started down the sidewalk to the truck. There was a man in it. At the same instant I saw him, he saw me. As I ran toward him, he jumped from the truck and disappeared into the woods behind the parking lot. Looking in the cab, I could see that he had broken the lock in the door and already had the steering column apart and was hot-wiring the ignition. In a few more seconds, he would have had it running and our truck would have been gone. From then on, I dismantled part of the truck's electrical system each night to keep thieves from stealing it.

What seemed to be the final blow to us came one day in the form of a report from one of our new Basotho friends. We had begun meeting on Sundays with a small group of Basotho in Maseru who were interested in the gospel. Their friends and relatives in some of the outlying villages wanted to hear this message as well. Consequently, we began making trips to conduct services in these areas. One day our friend brought word to us that some people were growing resistant to our preaching from the Bible and threats were now being circulated. In addition, some of the opposition planned to report us to the Ministry of Interior and demand that legal action be taken against us. Because we were visitors and not legal residents, their charges stood a strong chance of being sustained. From that day, we lived in fear that at any moment I might be picked up by the police and we would be expelled from the country.

Our prayers became intense as we asked God to preserve His Mission and spare us this danger. Missouri Baptists were joining intently with us in this plea. Pressure increased as we continued to hear little bits of news about the opposition and their activities. For weeks we lived with this tension. Then one day in the mail I found a brown paper envelope from the immigration office. We were ordered to bring our passports and report to the office within 48 hours. We had heard of this kind of action in other countries, and it always meant that an expulsion order had been issued.

How could this be happening? After all God had done to bring this Mission into being, we were more and more confused at His apparent lack of response to our pressing needs. Why were the prayers of the large group of intercessors being ignored when He was the One Who had called them? We were sick. We were depressed and fatigued. And now it looked as if we were also out.

The next day as I dressed, I wondered why all of this had happened. Walking up Kingsway to the immigration office I felt like a man going to his own execution. When an immigration official came to speak to me, I showed him the letter. Taking the reference number from it, he went to the files. Before long he returned with a document that looked like an official order. I waited for the final blow.

"I have here, Rev. Sprinkle, instructions from my government for the issuance of your resident visa."

7

Be Still

The end of July was freezing cold, yet I was sweating. Standing in the cold, dimly-lit hall of a stone government building awaiting my appointment with officials from the registrar's office, I thought, *What irony.* The reversed seasons of the Southern Hemisphere meant that in Lesotho we were experiencing the cold of winter. So why was I sweating as if I were back in a Missouri July? I realized as I nervously waited in the unheated building that it was the situation, not the season, that was affecting me.

"Rev. Sprinkle, we are ready for you. Please come in."

This was it. The three months of work on the constitution and its supporting documents, the weekly meetings with the lawyer who was an expert in Lesotho law, and the numerous preliminary talks with registrar officials were now behind me. Today, in these next few minutes, I would receive the final decision of the registrar of societies regarding our application for the legal establishment of the Baptist Mission in Lesotho.

Looking across the table at the two women, I thought I detected a negative aura about their manner and demeanor. I couldn't be sure and I certainly didn't want to believe it. The ranking official began to speak.

"As you know, Rev. Sprinkle, we look very carefully at the applications of any new organizations which request permission to operate in Lesotho. Your documents are well prepared, and we have considered all of your justifications and explanations. Unfortunately, we have several major objections. I'm sorry, but your application has been denied."

Now, when I should have been sweating, I was instead calm and intensely focused. I saw in a flash the ramifications if this decision remained final. We might be able to stay in the country but without an organization to which we were officially related, we would not be able to project and expand work, and we would likely be unable to bring in any other missionaries to work with us. We weren't being put out. We were being locked in. No Mission would emerge. No future would unfold. No Baptist churches would blanket the mountains and valleys of this beautiful land. I knew this wasn't God's will, and I was unwilling to settle for it.

This was not the first time a gate had been slammed shut in my face. In learning how to honor Christ in my everyday work, I had developed a principle for dealing with the problem I now faced. "When the gate in the wall is closed, don't try to batter it down and walk over it. Move laterally along the wall and look for another opening."

With this in mind, I began to move along the wall. "Could you please list for me the objections on which you are basing your decision?"

Moving through the list with them, I soon realized two things: the objections were not several, and they were not major. Point by point, I addressed their concerns and provided rationale for each item in the documents that they were questioning. One objection in particular seemed to be a Catch-22. They did not want to register an organization numbering only two members, and yet they admitted, at my pressing, that it was highly unlikely we would be able to bring in other missionaries to join the Mission unless it were first legally registered.

Their last objection involved a small village church in the north of the country that had in its name the word *Baptist*. This church had been registered at some time in the past, and although the office was not even sure it still was in existence, they maintained that it presented an insurmountable barrier to registration.

I had never heard of this particular church, but I knew that during the last 30 years, literally thousands of indigenous African churches had come into being. The origin of most of these revolved around people who had been told in a dream to start a church that would teach the "real" truth. The names chosen for many of these churches included denominational names used in an incongruous mix such as the Holy Universal Methodist Catholic Episcopal Church of the Holy Mountain. One in particular that I remembered even had the subtitle the One True Apostate Church!

We talked about this phenomenon and the fact that the names chosen for these churches normally had nothing to do with the beliefs associated with the denominations whose names were co-opted. I could see, as in our discussions on the earlier points, that I was overcoming their objections. Yet I was not making headway in gaining a reconsideration of our application. Throughout the meeting I was careful to keep our discussion on a cordial and respectful level. In no way did I want these officials to think I was questioning their abilities or motives. It became clear to me that they were determined, for reasons which I was unable to ascertain, to keep the Baptist Mission out of Lesotho.

So far I had found no openings in the wall. I had noticed one thing during the meeting, however, which seemed odd. The official who did most of the talking periodically glanced at the other person for what I judged to be support. I decided to probe a bit and I found the opening through which the Baptist Mission might pass. I learned, as the officials grew increasingly uneasy with my questions, that the actual head of this office was on vacation and they were acting in her place while she was away. The moment I learned this, I requested an appointment with the higher official.

A blast of winter wind blew my coat open as I walked from the building. I barely noticed. My mind was locked on one thought: next Monday, August 3, 2:00 P.M. We had another chance. We had the appointment.

Back in the disco flat, Nancy and I committed ourselves to intensified prayer over the next four-and-one-half days.

While we were thankful for the additional time to ask God for a reversal of the decision, we lamented our inability to alert the Missouri intercessors of our need. The three Missouri/Lesotho communications channels available to us each had limitations which rendered them useless in this situation.

Our normal vehicle for communicating prayer needs and answers was Missouri *PrayerWays,* a monthly prayer guide that included a daily prayer item from Lesotho. Missouri WMU published this guide and sent it to every Missouri Baptist who desired it. Nancy and I continually made notes on developments and needs, sending them in monthly letters to Marilyn Coble, the state WMU prayer coordinator.

Prayerfully, Marilyn arranged and organized the requests and answers. From the time we posted the monthly requests to Marilyn until they were printed, mailed, duplicated at the associational level, and then actually arrived in the hands of the intercessors took two months. *PrayerWays* was our frontline weapon in the prayer partnership; but in immediate needs situations like this one, its built-in time lag rendered it useless—or so we thought.

This limitation of the monthly prayer guide had concerned us from the beginning of the partnership. One of the ways Missouri WMU compensated was to purchase and present us with a video camera. Alberta generously promised, "Film video prayer letters to us whenever you need to and send them back. We'll duplicate them and get them out to the pray-ers as soon as possible."

Not only had these video letters proven to be effective and faster communication tools, they carried an added benefit. The usefulness of the printed *PrayerWays* was enhanced as the intercessors began to develop a visual picture of Lesotho, her people, and the countryside. We had just prepared a video the week before our application was denied. In it we had stressed the critical need for the Mission's registration; however, the video was still in the mail somewhere and no help could come from this source before Monday.

This left us with only one final option: the telephone.

Unfortunately, we did not have one. The few pay phones available were basically useless for making overseas calls. Lesotho's telephone system was being upgraded and eventually reliable direct dialing was to be available. For now, however, the system was intermittent and undependable. The Holzes had earlier offered us the use of their phone, and we had tried it, but it had taken as long as a week just to get a call through to Johannesburg. Someday the phone would be very useful to the Mission, but not yet. Our best reasoning told us that in this, the most critical hour in the Mission's short history, we would be left to stand alone. Frankly, this distressed us. We felt isolated and in a vacuum.

We were alone, but not alone. We spent the next few days in prayer and preparation for the meeting with the registrar. Even as I worked, my confidence, strangely, was not growing. I knew I had been well prepared for the first meeting and, although I now knew the exact objections and could prepare specifically to answer them, I remained uncertain that I could carry the day. Somehow I felt my preparation was for naught.

Toward the end of the weekend I had a vague, then growing, reminder of words from Psalm 46:10 KJV: "Be still, and know that I am God." There was no further or fuller word— just, "Be still." He did not show us the outcome of the meeting. He gave us no vision of the future. The word was, "Trust Me," and we did.

Compounding the pressure on us during these days was the lack of visible movement toward a resolution of our housing problem. The disco flat and our housing options continued to be as bad as ever. Two or three times I learned of houses with some initial promise, only to see the promise evaporate and the houses go instead to international companies. I suspected an old problem was cropping up again. A month or so later, my suspicions were confirmed.

I had followed up a lead and contacted an organization with a house for lease. We viewed the house and found it was ideal. Its three bedrooms and fenced yard looked perfect. I told the agent we would take it. She said she needed a few days to draw up the lease and told me where to pay the deposit and sign the lease. We were ecstatic. Finally, we had a home. We couldn't wait to tell the Missourians.

On the appointed day I went to the office and asked for the man I was told to see. I was prepared to pay the necessary fees and sign the lease. But instead of taking my money, he was evasive and noncommittal. Eventually, he ended the conversation by saying, "The lease isn't quite ready. I'll need a little more time."

When the same scenario was played out in my next meetings with the man, I was sure what the problem really was. I checked my suspicions with two friends who had been in Lesotho much longer than I, and they confirmed my fears. Only a bribe would produce a lease. This was not a new problem to us and I responded according to our standing convictions: We would not do what was illegal or unethical to accomplish God's work, regardless of what the local custom might be. The house went to someone else.

Our outlook for housing was totally bleak. We had only one encouraging development since we had come into the country. In June, Dave Blomberg, the director of Mission Aviation Fellowship in Lesotho, had offered us the house in which the Holzes were living while they were on furlough from late July through early January. With gratitude, we accepted his offer. We were struck by the sweet irony in this episode.

This was not the first time we had met Dave Blomberg. In the early 1980s we had been on a rare trip from our village in the northern Ngamiland region of Botswana to Johannesburg on business. While we were visiting there, a new missionary family had flown in and was put in the other bedroom of the Baptist guest house in which we were staying. Their names were Dave and Kathy Blomberg.

Since they were new to the area, we showed them around and helped them get oriented to Johannesburg as we went about our business. I was in missions aviation for our Baptist Mission in Botswana at that time as well, so I was able to introduce Dave to some contacts at the airports in Johannesburg that would be helpful to him later.

As we left the city to begin the long trip back to our village, we were thankful for the unexpected blessing in helping these new missionaries get started. We never expected to see them again.

But now, years later, here was Dave Blomberg helping us get established in a new country!

While we made preparation to move to the Holzes' house, I continued to look for permanent housing. The ideal situation for us would have been to buy a house or a residential lot on which we could build. Renting was acceptable on a temporary basis, but ideally we wanted to put funds into a home the Mission would own. As moving day, July 27, was approaching, I received word from an intermediary that he had located a lot.

"Nancy!" I exclaimed as I walked into the house. "This could be it." Her eyes looked for some reason to hope that this time might finally bring something substantive.

"I've learned of a lot up on the hill behind us that is *definitely* for sale." My stress on the word *definitely* brought a flicker of response from Nancy.

"This one really is for sale?" Her eyes were searching for confirmation. Too many times already word of property supposedly for sale had raised false hopes in us.

"Yes, the owner wants to sell his lot. I've already made an appointment for us to see it."

Later, as the owner's agent rode with us, giving directions as we went, we wondered if this might finally be the one. Pulling off the road at the place he indicated, we found ourselves looking at a lot in an area of scattered houses. The lot was small and barren, but it was adequate, and it was for sale. Walking across it, I asked about the price.

"You can see that this is a very nice lot. Lots like this are very hard to come by. I'm not sure about cost, but the owner did mention the 10,000 to 12,500 US dollar range."

The price was outrageous, and both of us knew it. We also both knew that market pressure was driving prices steadily higher. The agent waited.

"That price is much too high for this property, but I am interested. Go ahead and set an appointment with the owner. I would like to begin negotiations."

While we moved, we prayed about this lot and awaited a word. When it came, it wasn't good. The owner had decided to hold on to the site. With the market going as it was, he might eventually receive twice his current asking price. The little boost that we received by having the Holzes' house to live in for a few months was immediately dispelled by the growing hopelessness of the housing scene. Increasingly, we understood that only by a miracle would we get a Mission residence in Maseru.

During the first week of June, we had airmailed the monthly list of prayer requests and answers to Marilyn Coble. She received them about two-and-a-half weeks later and began sorting and editing them for what would become the August 1987, Missouri *PrayerWays*. To Marilyn, this was not just an editorial job. She prayed as she worked, asking God to guide her selection and arrangement of the daily Lesotho prayer items. When the August master was completed, she sent it to Jefferson City for printing, duplicating, and mailing. Although we were on the mailing list, July came without our receiving our August *PrayerWays*. We weren't concerned. Even using airmail, our US letters usually took two to three weeks to arrive. The important point was that we knew the intercessors already had their prayer guides. Ours would be here any day now.

Monday morning, August 3, was a typical Lesotho winter day with clear bright skies and a cold crisp wind blowing off the mountains. After lunch I prepared to return to the registrar of societies for my 2:00 P.M. meeting.

Standing in the same hall where I had stood the week before, I waited to be called into the director's office. Yes, I was sweating again. Finally, she opened her door and invited me in. I sat down in the well-worn wooden chair she indicated. She went around and sat behind her desk. Her only words were those of a brief greeting that revealed nothing to me. Then she sat quietly in front of me, looking down at what I recognized to be the stack of documents I had prepared with our application. I could not see exactly what she was reading at the moment, but I suspected it was the report of the two officials I had met the week before.

After three or four minutes of silence, during which I waited and wondered what she could possibly be thinking, she raised her eyes over the papers that she held in front of her and spoke. "Rev. Sprinkle, I have reviewed all of the documents associated with your Mission and the application for legal registration here in Lesotho. Frankly, I must tell you that I find no merit in . . ."

Her face betrayed no emotion. She was speaking with measured steadiness. I suddenly recognized in myself a rising sense of doom. She was going to say, "I find no merit in your application. Your request is denied." It was over. Somehow the Mission hadn't made it. I thought all of this in an instant, between her words. She, though, had not stopped speaking, and now I heard the rest of her statement.

"I find no merit in any of the objections."

I held onto the arms of the chair. She was rejecting the recommendations of her own employees and co-workers. She was granting her approval for the establishment of the Baptist Mission in her country. Before I could think of anything to say, she was signing the necessary papers. In a moment it was done. Our petition for legal recognition was approved! Weeks of administrative time would still be necessary for the documents to travel to the appropriate offices for recording, stamping, and issuance of the official document. That was immaterial. I didn't care how long the rest of the administrative work took. We could wait. The important thing was we were approved.

Then the official asked a surprising question of me. "Do you have a few minutes?"

I couldn't imagine why she would ask, but I responded, "Yes, of course."

She got up from her desk, carrying our file, and without a word left me sitting alone in her office. I spent the ten minutes she was gone in rushing praise and thanksgiving to God. I hadn't done a thing. I hadn't even had an opportunity to speak. All of my preparation for detailed and difficult negotiations was unnecessary. I had been merely a spectator.

When the official finally reentered the office, she was carrying a bound folder of documents. It contained the final constitution and bylaws of the Baptist Mission of Lesotho. She had gone throughout the government building and in a few minutes taken care of all the other needed details. She placed the folder in my hands. On its front cover I saw the most beautiful picture I think I will ever see. There, in all its official blandness, was the stamped seal of the nation of Lesotho. The Baptist Mission of Lesotho, which had been conceived in heaven, gestated in the hearts of Missouri Baptists, and birthed by a whole host of prayer parents now officially existed.

When I recovered my voice, I thanked this woman profusely for her kindness. "It's my pleasure," she replied. Then as I was about to open her office door to leave, she stopped me with another question.

"Tell me, Rev. Sprinkle, where is it that you are living here in Maseru?"

That's an odd question, I thought as I answered, "We've had much difficulty in locating housing here in the city. Currently, we are staying in the home of friends while they are in the States, but we must find something permanent before they return in January."

"What exactly are you looking for?"

"We will take just about anything to be able to stay in the country, but ideally we would like to buy a house or a lot where we could build a house."

She looked at me for a moment and then asked, "Do you have another minute?"

At this stage, I would have gladly waited the rest of the day just to see what else God might be doing. I returned to the chair and sat down.

Looking through her phone book for a number she said, "Some months ago I heard of a lot for sale. Let me see if I can reach a friend of mine who is a lawyer and will know the details."

Dialing a number, she was soon in conversation with her friend. She paused, turned to me, and inquired, "The lot is available. Are you interested?"

"Yes, I definitely am. Can you get me an appointment to see it?"

With the completion of the call, we had the appointment and a part in a most amazing story. This lot had originally been sold in an estate sale. The buyer had made a down payment and then for some reason never followed through on the sale's contract. The time had expired and the papers had just come back onto the attorney's desk with instructions for resale of the lot. He had not had time to do anything with it until the call came from his friend at the Registrar of Societies.

Later, when we met at the lot, I saw that it was large, in a good area, and quite nice. When I asked him the price, he was at first puzzled. "I don't know," he replied, thinking about my question. "It was sold at auction. I suppose if you would be willing to match the sale price that should be adequate."

"What was that price?" I asked, fearing the worst.

"The sale price was about $3,000. You can have it for that."

Today our residence and the office of the Baptist Mission of Lesotho stand on this lot.

Of course, I didn't know all of this that miraculous day back in the registrar's office as I stood to leave. My repeated thanks to the official for her help were very inadequate. She could not know the magnitude of what she had done for us and for the future of the Mission. As I was about to open her door to go into the hall, my curiosity won out and I had to ask, "How did you know about our housing problems since you do not know me?"

"Some time ago my husband was walking downtown with a friend when they met you on the sidewalk." When she told me the name of her husband's friend, I remembered the meeting. I had greeted this Mosotho friend and, in the course of our brief conversation, he had introduced me to his companion. I did not remember the man's name and I had not seen him since.

"After you parted, your friend told my husband that you could not find a place to live. Later at our home, my husband mentioned you and your situation to me. When I saw your Mission's application, I recognized your name and remembered the story. I also remembered that you were very kind to my husband."

Outside in the truck, I could hardly believe, I could barely comprehend, all that had transpired in the last half hour.

The meeting had been a historical confluence of circumstances and prearranged events that had resulted in a miraculous breakthrough for the Mission and the cause of Christ in this nation. After the great difficulty that had characterized every step forward for the Mission and for us, this was beyond comprehension. The two gravest situations that we faced, the issues that threatened our very future and effectiveness in this country, had been swept away in a rush that was almost too fast to follow. All I had done was sit in a chair and receive. Someone Else had won the day. How I wished that the intercessors could have witnessed this with me.

Driving home, I could barely wait to tell Nancy all the news. I made a quick stop at the post office to pick up our mail and then drove to the Holzes' house. Nancy was anxiously waiting for me in the yard. I held up the folder like a trophy. Then pointing to the official seal on the front, I exclaimed, "You're not going to believe the story I'm about to tell you!"

Those next moments were some of the finest that we have ever shared together as missionaries. The day had actually been a microcosm of what much of mission service in general is: long periods of struggle and sometimes even deep pain punctuated by points of indescribable glory. That yard became, in those moments, a great cathedral, as high praise rose from our hearts. God, in power, had visited us. We didn't know why He had chosen this moment. We couldn't explain it. We simply recognized it and rejoiced in it.

When we finished talking, I could not bring myself to go inside and sit down. I told Nancy to go on and I would stay out for a while. Opening the gate to the side garden, I walked in among the plants. I really had no purpose in being there, except to be alone for a few moments to consider what had just transpired. Never had I experienced anything like this. To see the results of God's work and view the key events He had scripted to make these breakthroughs possible was marvelous.

As I reviewed the details of the meeting over and over in my mind, I became aware that Nancy was calling me. Seeing me in the garden, she came toward the fence where we met. In her hand she held a small folded sheet of paper. "I just found in today's mail the new Missouri *PrayerWays* for August."

Handing it to me, she said, "Look at the statewide prayer request for today, August 3."

I read the request which thousands of intercessors had been taking before God on this day. "Pray that the government of Lesotho will approve the Baptist Mission as a legally registered organization."

Now I understood! As I had stood alone in that cold hall, waiting to go to the most important meeting of my life and the life of the Mission, I had not been standing alone. My meeting had been scheduled for 2:00 P.M. Two o'clock in the afternoon in Lesotho was 7:00 A.M. in Missouri. While I waited nervously to go in and plead with the registrar on behalf of the Mission, others on the other side of the world were pleading as well. All across Missouri in farmhouses, in bedrooms, in apartments, in kitchens, women and men were starting their day by first going before God on our behalf. They didn't know what I was facing at that very moment. Marilyn Coble didn't know, as she typed the August *PrayerWays*, what a critical day August 3 would be. God saw it all and orchestrated a focused concert of prayer for a moment in time, that His great willingness might be liberated to manifest in Lesotho the very desires of His heart.

I had been privileged to witness this miraculous day. More important, the Missouri intercessors had been privileged to have a part in bringing it to pass.

8

Gathering Darkness

"Tomorrow is our birthday, and we have received more mail this week than at any time in our lives," I wrote in my journal on August 19, 1987. My mind flashed back over the past few days to scenes in the post office. Since boxes were unavailable for rent, our MAF friends graciously were allowing our mail to be sent to their post office box. Now, though, a problem had developed. The postal clerks couldn't get all our mail into the box. Each day we had to call at the counter for our mail. The scene became embarrassing when other postal patrons stared at me as the clerk handed over stack after stack of letters.

The volume of mail wasn't what most impressed me that day, though, as I continued writing. "More so than at any time in my life I sense the power of and answers to all the prayers of Missouri Baptists."

August had been the high point of an otherwise very difficult and depressing first four months in Lesotho. Our hope, as Nancy and I came to our shared birthday of August 20, was that this was also the turning point for us in Lesotho. We were enjoying the quiet and space of the Holzes' house after our three months in the disco flat. Our nonstop series of sicknesses seemed to be coming to an end. The wonderful answers to prayer in the face of what could have been disasters were strong encouragements. The group of believers with whom we met in Maseru now called themselves the Maseru Baptist Fellowship; and out in three villages we had established regular preaching points. To top off these victories, on August 30 I was planning to preach my first sermon in Sesotho. We had good reason to hope and believe we had weathered the long first storm and smoother sailing lay ahead.

The month of September was to show, however, that our hopes were not to materialize. We were not entering a new period of peaceful progress. We were descending into a darkening valley of debilitating struggle and physical decline. We would still progress but at an increasing cost.

The month began with good news and bad news. We needed somewhere to live between January 1988, when we had to leave the Holzes' house, and late 1988, when construction on a Mission house might be completed. On September 3 we learned that a rental house which might have filled this need was not going to be available. The news was disturbing but not overly so. It was just another disappointment which joined a growing list. On this same day, I took a phone call from a British man named Ron Pitter. As I listened to him, I saw again the familiar pattern of God's engineering circumstances to meet our needs.

Ron and I had never met, but this was not a great hindrance for God. His wife, Doreen, had met Nancy at a women's Bible study, and they had prayed about our critical housing need. Doreen mentioned this to Ron. He was the head of a large insurance company in Lesotho and an Anglican who was experiencing a deepening of His walk with Christ. A few days earlier he had been convicted of the command to help the brethren. In this context, God brought us and his company's vacant apartment to mind. As he prayed for guidance, God assured him that this indeed was his opportunity for ministry. Ron called and offered the apartment to us as a step of obedience in his own growing commitment to Christ. It was an answer to prayer for us.

An eager Sprinkle family met Ron's assistant at the apartment a few days later. The fourplex building we viewed was built on the side of a steep hill which required an unusual design to make the two-bedroom apartments usable. The company's flat was on three levels with a full set of steps between each level. We had never seen so many steps in a small apartment before, but this home would fill our next housing need. We told the man we would take it. Ron was planning to return to Great Britain in a few weeks. Before he left, he made sure the lease was prepared and signed. We appreciated his faithfulness to the Lord and the blessing it was to us. Later, we talked about all the steps in the apartment and joked about how running up and down them every day would be great physical conditioning. Had we been able to see into the next few weeks, we would not have been joking.

On the last day of the month, September 30, I crossed the Caledon River to keep an appointment with our physician, Dr. Strauss, in Ladybrand. I had begun having so much pain in both of my legs that I was experiencing difficulty in walking and driving our truck. In the meantime, Nancy and the boys had developed strep throat and a virus that completely incapacitated all three of them for several weeks. The strep infection itself was so painful that the boys cried almost continuously.

After the examination, Dr. Strauss told me that he thought I probably had tendinitis in my legs. An orthopedic specialist would be in Ladybrand the next week for a clinic, and he wanted me to see him. I was to stay off my feet as much as possible and come back the next week. During that week, I developed the same illnesses as the rest of the family. We all had to go back to the doctor again the next week.

We left Dr. Strauss that next week with antibiotics for each of us. I left the orthopedic surgeon with a troubling diagnosis. He suspected that my leg pain, which had worsened over the past week, was not actually caused by a problem in my legs but in my back. In ten days I was to travel to the South African city of Bloemfontein, a one-and-one-half-hour drive west of Maseru. Outpatient tests there would determine if his suspicions were correct.

By early November all of these test results were back from the laboratories and the cause of my problems was clear. Damage to the discs and vertebrae in my lower spine was creating pressure on the nerves that ran into my legs. My leg problem was indeed a back problem. I was sent back to Maseru with prescriptions and was ordered to bed for three weeks to see if the inflammation in my legs and lower back could be reduced.

Lying in bed for the rest of November, I reviewed what had transpired through September and October. After what appeared to be an end of sickness in late August, my family had been seriously ill for all of the next two months. Nancy, while sick, had continued to work as much as she could so that I could continue traveling and preaching. Because of her lupus, her normal reserves of strength were limited and now this extreme effort had left her with deep physical and mental exhaustion.

Crime and violence were escalating in Maseru. Always we had been careful, but now even daytime shopping trips were taking on an atmosphere of danger. In the third week of September, I had gone to the OK Grocery Store, located in the small open-air mall in the heart of Maseru. As I approached the store, I saw a crowd of people standing around the entrance of a small curio shop across from the store entrance. Spying a friend in the crowd, I asked about the gathering. The story he related to me illustrated the level that danger had reached in the city.

Maria, the woman who operated the shop and to whom we had spoken on several occasions, had been accosted by four men who had entered her shop during the busy lunch hour. While shoppers hurried by outside, the men tied Maria up, taped her mouth, and then fatally cut her throat with a knife. Her killers took a few inexpensive items with them as they left the shop and vanished among the noonday crowds. The apartment we had rented and would soon occupy was just behind this shopping area.

My illness meant that Nancy was forced to go alone to shop, do Mission business, work at the office, and take Matthew back and forth to school. Even before I had been put to bed, driving had become difficult for me. Our truck with its four-wheel drive capabilities was ideal for mountain travel, but its stiff suspension system caused each bump on the roads and trails to be jarring and painful. Gradually, I had been limiting my travel. It seemed the Enemy had been increasing his activity. Each of the groups of believers in Maseru and the outlying villages was experiencing problems and persecutions, and I could only lie on my back and pray for them.

In one village, vandals harassed the little group of believers whenever they met to talk and pray. In another, a drunken brawl resulted in the murder of one of the men of the village and scared the women of the little Baptist congregation so much that they were afraid to meet.

In Maseru, my absence provided the opportunity for a man to come in and attempt to take over leadership of Maseru Baptist Fellowship. The man's forcefulness cowed the believers and lay pastor. Finally, at the end of a service one morning, the man announced that the next Sunday he would be preaching and that he would baptize the new believers who were awaiting baptism. This report was brought to me on Monday. I spent the rest of the week agonizing in prayer for the church. We do not know what transpired with the man that week, but on Sunday he did not show up and, thankfully, the crisis passed.

Seemingly, in every area of our work and our lives, we were experiencing debilitating problems. Only one area seemed to prosper during this difficult time. The believers, while disturbed and pressed, remained basically faithful and ultimately were strengthened. One instance in particular, brought light to these dark months and epitomized the faith and faithfulness of the little groups of believers.

In October, a woman named 'Mme Roberte from the mountain village of Canana gave this testimony. ('Mme is pronounced May and roughly translates as Mrs.) She had been an alcoholic in her village and had joined with others in cursing and mocking us each week when she saw our truck crawling up the mountain to the neighboring village of Masireletsa. Gossip told her and her friends that we were "Bible" preachers, and because I was white, they thought I was a South African. She knew that she should hear us preach for herself, but she refused. Her ridicule continued until the day we turned off the road and drove up to the hut of the chieftainess of Canana.

Along with the lay pastor of Maseru Baptist Fellowship and two of the women of the congregation, I asked the chieftainess if we could come in and speak to her about God and His love for her. She agreed. After admitting us into her hut, she left her door standing open. As one of the others spoke, I noticed a passing woman stop and then ease closer to the door. She stood outside for a minute or two, and then bowing and asking pardon from the chieftainess, she laid her shawl on the dirt floor just inside the doorway of the hut and sat to listen with rapt attention.

When we finished speaking, we asked the chieftainess if she would pray with us and accept Jesus as her Saviour. She reminded me of Paul's hearers in Athens as she said she "would hear us again about this Jesus." (Later this chieftainess did receive Christ and has since been very helpful in obtaining land for a church site in her village.) At this point, however, the woman on the floor spoke up, boldly declaring that she wanted to accept Jesus. Together we bowed, and 'Mme Roberte, the mocker of Christ and His servants, became in that moment a lover of Christ and one of His servants.

A few weeks later when opposition forced us out of Masireletsa, 'Mme Roberte said, "From now on you will come to my house." The little group of believers moved down the mountain to Canana and still meets in this woman's home. 'Mme Roberte herself became the pillar of the congregation and is a strong and unwavering witness to the Saviour.

In other countries where we have served, Baptists were sometimes referred to as People of the Book because of our unceasing preaching and teaching of the Bible. 'Mme Roberte's faithfulness resulted in a new name for Baptists in her region of Lesotho. Word began to spread of this woman and her unshakable faith in God. People in remote villages heard of her faith and traveled to her home when they had sickness or severe problems. She was a powerful believer in prayer and in God's love and power. She would always witness to all who came to her, as well as pray for them and their needs. God answered her faithful prayers, and before long this little congregation of Baptists who met in 'Mme Roberte's home were referred to all over the mountains as the People Who Pray. How fitting, it seemed, that believers back in Missouri, who truly were people who pray, had prayed into being this little Baptist congregation in the Lesotho mountains.

More than once I thought of 'Mme Roberte and her testimony as I lay in bed through the month of November. I thought of her praying for me and of all the Missourians who also were interceding for me. I should have been encouraged, but I was not. I wasn't getting better. As I realized that fact, my confusion and distress grew. Nancy reflected this as she watched me for encouraging signs and instead saw only decline.

The first days of rest had seemed to help somewhat. Then I began to have pain again that slowly increased as the days passed. To make matters worse, an old neck injury began to flare up. In 1980 I had been a passenger in a small plane when the pilot lost control during a difficult landing and crashed. The plane cartwheeled following the violent impact with the ground, and I was left hanging upside down in the wreckage with a damaged neck, right shoulder, and arm. In the years following the crash, I had experienced pain periodically whenever I drove extensively on the rough bush trails, but never the kind of pain I was experiencing now. As I lay there those weeks, with pressing family and Mission needs all around me, I thought over and over, *Why is this coming back with such a vengeance right now when I've got more than I can take care of already?*

On November 30 Nancy drove me back to Bloemfontein for a follow-up appointment with the specialist. He told us what we already knew. My condition was worsening. He gave me two additional medicines, one a stronger painkiller, and an appointment to enter the National Hospital in Bloemfontein the following Monday for more extensive tests and probably surgery on my spine.

The physical pain during that week of waiting was surpassed only by the mental and emotional anguish under which I suffered. I was powerless to care for the two most important responsibilities of my life: my family and the Mission—both critically needed me.

We had such big plans for this week. Giving them up intensified my sense of the Mission's needs. On Saturday, December 5, the lay pastor of Maseru Baptist Fellowship and our language tutor were to be married. This was going to be the first Baptist wedding in the country, and I was to officiate. Even through my earlier weeks of bedrest, I had continued preparation for the marriage, praying and believing that I would be up and able by wedding day. Now I had to call and tell them they would have to get another minister. They understood; I didn't.

Each day as I watched my wife struggle to care for me and the boys, I was tormented by what I saw happening to her. The burden of all that we had been through was excessive, even when we could face it together. Now the load was hers alone, and I could see it was too much. I didn't want to acknowledge the telltale signs I was seeing in her. Only in the next week could I force myself to write what I didn't want to admit. In my journal I wrote, "Nancy may have to go in the hospital herself as it seems her lupus is really giving her problems." A few months more would pass before we would know that my fears were grounded in fact. Her lupus was relapsing.

On Monday as she left me at the hospital, I feared for Nancy as she made the drive back to Lesotho alone. I felt that the effort of having to carry on alone back in Maseru might be too much. I prayed, *Oh God, lift her burdens and sustain her during this ordeal. She just can't take any more.* I wanted to believe that He would, but frankly, recent experience had left me wondering and in doubt.

Looking around the eight-bed ward in which I lay on this Pearl Harbor Day, I felt almost as if I had been transported back into the 1940s. The medical staff in the hospital was excellent, but the ward looked like ones I'd seen in World War II photo albums. The wicker-backed wheelchairs and the sisters' (nurses) earlier-era uniforms only added to this sense of time travel. As I began to move through my series of tests and examinations, I prayed for Nancy, wondering what she was facing.

On Wednesday morning at our hillside apartment in Maseru, Nancy heard a knock at the door. Looking out she saw Kathy Blomberg on the front porch. Nancy was glad to see a visitor and she invited Kathy in. As they sat down, Nancy noted that Kathy was nervous and upset. She obviously hadn't come by for a social visit. Visibly calming herself, Kathy told Nancy that she had just taken a call for us. (The Blombergs had offered us the use of their phone number as an emergency contact point for our families back in the States.) Nancy waited. Kathy held herself together until she came to the heart of the message. She broke as she said, "I'm sorry. Last night your dad died."

After Kathy left, Nancy sat alone while Stephen took his nap. She remembered her premonition of this before we left the US for Lesotho. We had planned that if her dad died, she would go home for the funeral and some additional time with her family. My being in the hospital made that impossible. As she cried alone in the silence of the apartment, she realized that she couldn't even reach me to tell me. She felt isolated and desperately alone. Where was God?

Seemingly, He was absent and uncaring at that hour. Actually, He was on His way. After lunch our friend Harris Waltner, pastor of the English-language Maseru United Church, and his wife, Christine, came by and spent time with Nancy. Nancy and Christine were close. The Waltners' presence was a channel of God's comfort and grace to her. Later that evening as Nancy sat on the front porch after putting the boys to bed, Dennis Preston, an Assembly of God friend and fellow missionary, stopped by. He had been in Bloemfontein that day on business and had come by to see me. He was stopping to give Nancy a report on my condition. When he learned what had happened, he stayed for an hour. He was another avenue through whom God ministered His love and care to Nancy. The next morning Nancy drove to Bloemfontein and brought me the news of her father's death.

On Saturday I was released from the hospital. The combined opinion of my team of doctors was that I had herniated discs in both my neck and my lower back. As the tests were not conclusive, they offered me the option of either exploratory surgery or traction. I felt that exploratory surgery on my spine was too risky. I was fitted with a traction device and sent home with orders to stay in bed for five weeks, spending eight hours per day in traction.

Lying on my back for eight hours each day with my vertebrae being stretched, I thought about the two areas of burden that had weighed so heavily upon me. I was more at peace about my family and their needs because of

God's personal care for Nancy during my week in the hospital. I still felt that I needed to be up and involved in helping Nancy and Matthew with their problems, but at the same time I felt assured that God would not leave them without help.

Regarding the Mission, though, my turmoil was even greater than it had been before I went into the hospital. On arrival back in Maseru, I was greeted with news of increasing problems for the congregations and additional difficulties in several ongoing Mission business matters. I was forced to face the fact that I was not doing my job and the Mission was suffering accordingly. I feared that our possible return to the States for my surgeries might prohibit our return. The Mission might then be closed. Even to consider this possibility caused me to feel torn apart inside.

I was a very depressed and troubled missionary on December 18, just one week before Christmas, when Presbyterian missionary Dick Dunkerton came by to visit. Dick was a veteran missionary to East Africa and an old friend of one of my missions professors at Southwestern Seminary, Earl Martin. When Earl had learned that we were going to Lesotho, he told me that his most recent letter from the Dunkertons had indicated they were moving from Tanzania to Lesotho. He told us to look them up when we arrived and wrote the Dunkertons to watch for us. We had found each other after we arrived and became fast friends. Dick and Barbara lived in the village of Morija and only occasionally came to Maseru. When Dick learned of our growing health problems, he came to see us.

As we talked, he sensed the heavy burden I was carrying for the young Mission and the possibility of its closing because of our inability to work. His keen insight enabled him to read between my words.

Finally, he spoke. "Randy, I understand your strong sense of responsibility and duty regarding the Mission and the new believers. It's good and right; but, you must balance it with one other fact. Ultimately, this Mission is God's."

Slowly his words penetrated the layers of pain and confusion that clouded my thinking. Ownership was not an issue for me, and that was not what I understood God to be reminding me in Dick's words. Rather the issue was responsibility. I was accountable for faithful stewardship of my time and life. God would care for this Mission and its people, either through me or through someone else. That was not my responsibility. My responsibility was to be faithful.

When Dick left, I wasn't any better physically, but I felt liberated. I could see clearly again. I could be faithful even if I were flat on my back. Through prayer I could be about my work. I was at peace. I was assured.

God would take care of His Mission.

9

Night and Light

Prayer guides our walk through both the light and the dark. I had been wandering, lost and disoriented, through a dark, deep cave. Dick's words were like the beam of a rescuer's light suddenly piercing the darkness. Everything around me remained dark, unlit. But the beam of God's word through His servant gave assurance: We were not alone, and we had a focal point for purposeful movement again.

To this point, our lives had grown slowly more confusing as declining health precluded our doing critical missions work. Now, although many of our questions remained unanswered, we had been given an orienting word from God. He was still ultimately involved in this Mission and our lives. By faith, we had known that. By circumstances, that faith was buffeted and shaken. Now by a new word, faith was bolstered and reanchored. Through prayer, we were walking in the light again.

My remaining weeks in bed, though, amply exposed us to the truth that the pray-er also walks through darkness. The light of God's will and His words to us illuminate our path. We can see the way well enough to walk in it. Very often, though, He does not light much of our surroundings. We do not see through the dimness to an understanding of our circumstances. There is darkness around us. With our eyes on the light, we walk faithfully through that which we cannot fully comprehend. When we turn from the light to focus on the confusing and seemingly contradictory signals of the world around us, we stop walking and sometimes even turn aside.

The intended walk of a believer is the walk of prayer. That is, it is a walk of trusting communion with God, informed, guided, and reassured by His responsive words. It is the walk that will allow us to advance successfully through life. The darkness that we, most assuredly, will face is a mixture of three general forms. One has as its source the Evil One, our Enemy, Satan, and is intended to deter and deceive us that we might be hindered and even destroyed.

A second form is that darkness which accompanies circumstances we do not fully understand. We may be strongly tempted to focus on these, to our detriment, because by their nature they appear to be contrary to what we expect God to be doing.

The third area of darkness is that of answered prayer not yet realized. Every prayer by a follower of Christ brings action by God. Experience may seem to contradict this. That is because most response by God is in the form of next-step preparation and progress rather than final-step victory. This process sometimes can take a very long time, and more often than not the believer cannot see what God is doing along the way in response to prayer. All seems to be darkness. The key word is *seems*.

As the middle of January 1988 passed, we returned to Bloemfontein for my follow-up evaluation. Again, the report was not good. The drive back to Lesotho was spent in sober discussions which came again and again to the same conclusion: I was going to have to have back and neck surgery. The surgeries could be performed at National Hospital in Bloemfontein, first on my lower back and a few months later on my neck. My prognosis was good, but one factor made the decision to move ahead impossible. Nancy's lupus had progressed to the point that caring for me and the responsibilities of the Mission would be extremely difficult for her during my months of recuperation. In fact, she needed an extended time of treatment and recuperation herself. We had only one option, yet we could not bring ourselves to acknowledge and consider it. We were going to have to leave Lesotho and return to the States on medical furlough.

I suppose that even in December God was trying to tell us this, but we couldn't believe it. Why, after all that had gone into establishing the Mission and the new congregations, must we now leave? How could God put together a vast network of intercessors and then seem powerless to remove physical conditions which threatened the very existence of the Mission He had called into being? He could heal us, and we could be back about our ministry. Our prayer partners were joining with us in fervently asking this of Him, but heaven was silent. It was not to be.

Sometime during this period, a new request began to make its way into our prayers. "If we are no longer to be the ones serving here, then bring someone else to take up the task." The articulation of this request, even in its formative stage, was not only a response of obedience from our pained hearts but also the channel for God to draw other lives into the Lesotho odyssey. Of course, we saw none of this. Darkness was swirling around us. We had only the thin beam of light to walk by: "This Mission is God's." That light was enough. We could trust, with assurance, that He would be taking care of His Mission.

And He was.

Lehurutshe lay hundreds of kilometers to the north in the South African homeland of Bophuthatswana. It was a typical southern African village with dusty trails and scattered houses. The land was semiarid and barren. All indications were that little would grow here, let alone flourish. That was until Stacy and Sheila Houser came to Lehurutshe. The Housers, with their two elementary school-age sons Andrew and Derek, had come out of Texas to this village of dryness. Stacy, a former pastor, was directing the Texas Baptist Encampment at Palacios, when, in 1985, God called them to Africa. Long before Texas, though, the Housers had known life and ministry in international settings. Both were MKs (missionaries' kids). Sheila was the daughter of Finley and Julia Graham and had grown up in the Middle East. Stacy, the son of Jim and Molly Houser, called East Africa home.

In the walking of their own pilgrimage along the path of God's will, they had come to this dusty village in one of the northern areas of a country, the name of which most of the world found impossible to pronounce: Bophu-thatswana. There they served willingly, faithfully witnessing and ministering, tilling the soil and planting the seeds that God then caused to grow. Both they and the Baptist church there flourished. Their ministry of evangelism and church development expanded as new opportunities in other villages came to their attention. They were faithful in their praying as well, and daily were lifting all of their lives and work before God for His blessing and guidance.

In the closing months of 1987, something strange began to happen in the Housers' lives. At first, only rarely, and then with growing frequency, their prayertimes were being invaded. As they sought to focus their praying on Lehurutshe and the nation of Bophuthatswana, they would hear in their mind's ear a distracting message. Initially, it was only a single word. It was the name of another country. It was the country where we were living and struggling: Lesotho. As with all who endeavor to be obedient in intercession, Stacy and Sheila had experienced the stray and distracting thoughts that come in prayer. With a discipline borne out of years of prayer, they put this new thought aside and proceeded to lift their concerns and responsibilities before God.

As the weeks passed, the frequency of this invading thought increased, though, until like the young boy Samuel of so long ago, they realized that this was the voice of God. They must listen. As they asked God to clarify for them these unusual thoughts about Lesotho, they began to talk together about what this might mean for them. The next few weeks brought the answer. Although the Housers knew nothing about Lesotho except that a missionary family from Botswana had been sent there to begin a new Mission, they came to the conviction that God intended them also to move to Lesotho and join this young Mission.

With His direction now clear, they called the Mission office in Johannesburg and made an appointment to meet with area director, John Faulkner, when he next traveled through the area in December. At that meeting, they shared with him how they had come to this conviction and requested a transfer to Lesotho, as scheduling permitted.

Transfers from country to country on the missions field do not happen quickly or without strong justification. Much time and expense go into a missionary becoming effective in a country and culture. Leaving this to start over in a new setting can only happen as God clearly directs. John listened as the Housers spoke. When they were finished, he affirmed them in what they understood to be God's voice. He then asked them to go back to their station and do two things: be faithful in the work God had sent them to do in Bophuthatswana and continue to pray for the working out of His will regarding them and Lesotho. After prayer together, the Housers returned to their station.

John Faulkner was left with one particularly moving thought. Never once had the Housers mentioned any reason or need for their transfer to Lesotho. They knew nothing about our health conditions and the precarious situation of the Mission. Alone in a distant village they were responding, not to a crisis situation in Lesotho but solely to the Spirit of God. This carried strong weight in John's thinking as he began himself to consider prayerfully the Housers' request and God's plan for Lesotho. He had been an early and strong supporter of the prayer partnership concept, and he knew that Missouri intercessors were at work. He had to acknowledge, as he went on with his trip, that he was seeing the product of their work.

John now had some vital inside information regarding God's care of and future plans for His Mission. Back in Lesotho, though, we did not, and the stress was becoming overwhelming.

Our physical pain during this period was exceeded only by the emotional pain which our approaching departure brought. Two aspects were producing the staggering burden. Somehow we were being forced by health to leave the country and ministry that God had prepared and where He had placed us. Was He powerless to intervene? We had to answer no. He was and is all-powerful. Had the channel for His intervention, prayer, been closed or neglected? Again, of course not. Not only were we praying but so were thousands of others, and God had been answering these prayers powerfully and miraculously. Why, then, were our health conditions unchanged? Why were we unable to do the work He had sent us to Lesotho to accomplish? Why did it seem that He was abandoning us? Only with much prayer did we come to a difficult faith conclusion.

Regardless of what the situation seemed to indicate, God remained actively and powerfully involved in our lives. His purposes for us were greater than the dominating press of the immediate. His refusal to heal us in answer to prayer was a response of love. To heal would be to diminish the wider impact of His complete will for and through us. The prayer lifted in faith always brings a positive response from God. The prayer of faith, though, always rests on and springs from the revealed will of God. Need, desire, emotion provide impetus, but not the basis, for answer.

We understood finally that God was hearing and answering countless prayers for the restoration of our health. He just was not answering as we thought best. The suffering was not to be removed. He had permitted these circumstances, and with our acceptance of them, His fuller desires could be realized. We were at peace, at last.

Linked to these personal struggles was the burden for the Mission which would, with our departure, be unstaffed and in danger of being closed. Through the days and nights of January, the conviction grew that John Faulkner might now be convinced that closure of the Baptist Mission of Lesotho was the only realistic option. We were determined to make every effort to prevent this. From our field associate, James Westmoreland, in Johannesburg, I learned John would next be in Johannesburg in February. Through James, I scheduled an appointment with both of them. I told him I wanted to brief them on the complete situation with the Mission before John made a decision regarding the Mission's future. Since I could not make the drive to Johannesburg, I next called Lesotho Airways and booked a seat on the flight which left the morning of my appointment.

I spent the remaining days preparing myself for the briefing and what I expected would be a plea for the future of the Mission. We knew John. We trusted and respected his walk with Christ; but, we weren't taking any chances. We also prepared him by unceasing prayer.

With the acceptance of our inability to continue the work in Lesotho and the beginning of definitive plans to return to the States for medical care, earlier words from a friend resurfaced. Suzanne Groce was the daughter of missionaries Doug and Evelyn Knapp of Tanzania. She, along with her husband, Lynn, had served through the developmental years of the Ethiopian Mission and had seen and experienced the struggles of pioneer missions work. They were our friends and had cried and prayed for us when we had been taken out of Ethiopia. When Suzanne learned of our transfer to Lesotho, she wrote to pledge their prayer support. Her letter included these words which, in the quiet evening darkness after the boys were in bed, would come repeatedly and haunt our thoughts.

"Starting work in a new country is not a glorious missionary adventure and has broken some good people."

We had too many years of experience ever to have believed that Lesotho would be a glorious adventure. We had not acquired enough insight, though, to foresee that we might be some of those who would be broken along the way.

Meeting day arrived, and the Fokker F-27 of Lesotho Airways took off from Maseru and turned on course, gaining altitude as it banked. My thoughts, as I looked down on Lesotho, were of my family I had just left behind. As the trip progressed, these same thoughts expanded to the larger family of believers behind me. They were our brothers and sisters and, in another way, our children. I reminded myself that these really were His children. I reminded Him of His words to us through Dick Dunkerton. This was His Mission. The churches and ministry and future for which it existed were solely and ultimately His. And I reminded Him that the future of His Mission was at stake in the meeting that lay only a few hours away.

As my plane winged its way north, I asked once again

that nothing vital to the manifesting of His will concerning Lesotho be overlooked. Although I was high above the earth and the day was clear, I could not see far enough ahead to see a car that was heading east toward Johannesburg. It had come from one of the homelands carrying two people. They too were praying and wondering—wondering what might come from the same meeting toward which I was heading.

I also could not see that God had answered our prayers. Nothing had been overlooked.

After checking into my room at the missionary guest house, I took some pain pills and lay down on the bed. I was sweating, but it was not from the tension and anticipation. This time it was from pain. As I rested quietly, I prayed that on this crucial day the pain in my back and neck would subside and not be the constant mental distraction that it had become.

With the arrival of the appointed time, I hobbled to the office building next door and met John and James. The meeting was long and, although I had to change chairs periodically because of my back, it went well. John had sketched an informal agenda which began with an update on our health and moved to reports on the churches, the outlook for future opportunities, a political overview of the country, and the status of all ongoing Mission business. The last item for discussion was whether another missionary family would be assigned.

Even as I began to speak, I was careful not to be too forceful. As strong as my feelings were on this point, I easily could have been overbearing. I reviewed all that God had done to establish the Mission—how He had opened the country, and how He had led us out of Botswana and into Lesotho. I then crowned my presentation with telling again the story of the Missouri/Lesotho Prayer Partnership. I stressed that while I could not explain the many problems and why we were having to leave, I could make one statement with total assurance. Rather than God being done with Lesotho, He was instead only just beginning.

"John," I said, "I believe that somewhere God has prepared a career couple for Lesotho and they are here on one of our fields right now. I don't think you should be

99

pondering whether to continue the Mission. What you need to do is find these missionaries and do what's necessary to send them in. I am convinced they are out there somewhere."

John Faulkner had been silent through this last and crucial part of the meeting. Now he looked at me with an expression I judged to be both wonder and amazement. After a long pause, he finally spoke.

"Randy, I have a couple over in the guest house right now waiting to talk to you, and they're waiting to talk to you about Lesotho."

10

A Future Hope

The sidewalk ran uphill in front of the line of rooms which comprised the Baptist guest house. I had run up this sidewalk many times. Today, when I wanted to run as never before, I had to settle for a slow, careful walk. The meeting had been too long and I was stiff. Noting the room numbers as I progressed, I wondered about the couple behind the next door. I knocked and stepped back. These were the missionaries for whom we had been praying. Here was God's own choice for future leadership of the Mission. *What will they be like?* I thought as I waited.

In only a moment I knew. An attractive young woman with curly blonde hair answered the door. When I introduced myself, she smiled, revealing inner beauty and joy. Behind her appeared a man, open and pleasant. Stacy and Sheila Houser invited me in. From the first minutes of talk across their kitchen table, I sensed an atmosphere of harmony and identification with God's purposes for Lesotho. Eventually, we moved outside into the sunshine and talked through the last hour of the afternoon. I asked about their pilgrimage and marveled to myself as they related the prayer experiences in the past months that had brought them to this hour.

They were hungry to know everything about Lesotho and the Mission. I took a break to lie down and rest for a while, and then we went to a local restaurant. There, over an extended dinner, I told them the story. I went back to a phone call in a mission house in Texas and told them all I knew about God and His plans for a little hidden mountain country called Lesotho. I told them how God had placed prayer in the preeminent place at each turn of the Mission's short history. In turn, they marveled as I shared about the Missouri/Lesotho Prayer Partnership. Their response was a familiar one to me: "What must God want to do in this country!" They experienced some of the gratitude and excitement we had felt as I shared the marvelous early victories in the country, and they became somber as I related our health situation and the plans that had been finalized just that afternoon. In a few weeks, we would be leaving Lesotho on medical furlough.

The knock on the door startled John Faulkner. He was just getting ready for bed. He glanced at his watch. It was 10:00 P.M. Who could be at his door? Opening it, he found an apologetic Stacy and Sheila Houser.

"We know it's late," they said, "but could we talk for a few minutes?" John invited them in. The hours of discussion with me through the afternoon and early evening had been followed by the Housers' own personal discussions alone in their room. Everything they had heard had only served to solidify and confirm to them that God was indeed calling them to Lesotho. They communicated this to John. The next step was his. By the following day when Stacy and Sheila began their trip back to Lehurutshe, another decision had been finalized. The Housers' transfer had been approved. They were on their way to Lesotho.

Their coming paralleled our leaving. Before leaving Johannesburg, I booked our flights back to the States. As I completed the arrangements, I was forced to face the fact that our "lifetime" of ministry in Lesotho would encompass only five more weeks. I spent the flight back to Maseru making a mental list of everything we had to do before leaving. Reviewing the list, I could see that it was going to be a very full five weeks.

We would have to close the Mission office and find storage for and move all of the office equipment and furniture. We would have to vacate our apartment and sell all of our furniture and appliances. We faced crating and shipping personal effects and tending to countless Mission business items. Most important, from a personal standpoint, were the meetings and visits with the numerous families and congregations with whom we worked. Naturally these friends were feeling a real sense of loss and fear about the future. These meetings were the most painful parts of our last days.

I discussed with the Basotho Christians why we were going and tried to help them understand the very difficult question of why God had not answered their prayers by healing us. They were encouraged by the news of the coming of the Housers. I tried to reassure them that God would take care of them. Frankly, I desperately needed encouragement myself as I struggled with the reality that I would probably never see these people again here on earth. Anguish surrounded the farewell prayers with each group.

One unusual aspect of these final weeks was the coming of a film crew from the Foreign Mission Board. The Board was very committed to the prayer partnership concept and had planned a television special about the Missouri/Lesotho endeavor. This crew was on an extended trip through Africa and earlier had scheduled to come and spend a few days with us. When we had agreed, we had not known that we would be in the middle of packing. The filming went very well in spite of the time demands. The crew later traveled to Missouri to film the stateside account. The final program aired over religious cable networks as a beautiful presentation of the story.

Since Stacy and Sheila were due to return to the States in about six or seven months for furlough, John Faulkner decided that they should remain in Lehurutshe and complete their work there rather than move immediately to Maseru. During these last months before their planned furlough in October, however, they could make monthly weekend trips to Lesotho. Their visits would give continuity to the ministry there.

In correspondence with the Housers, we arranged a time when they could travel to Maseru for the first long weekend. We introduced them to the various church leaders and briefed them on everything concerning the Mission and its work. One item that demanded immediate attention if the Housers were to have a place to live, was the building of a Mission house on the lot we had acquired. We had already made contact with an architect and a home builder in Maseru. Stacy and Sheila worked with these men and got the Mission home under construction before they left on furlough.

They also picked up our initial work, constituting the Maseru Baptist Fellowship into a church. From May through July 1988, they worked diligently in meetings and conferences with the congregational leaders to prepare a constitution. They understood the great importance of this first Baptist church constituted in Lesotho and the pattern it would set for the others that would follow. They worked thoroughly and well. On August 28, 1988, the Maseru Fellowship became Maseru Baptist Church. This high day in the history of the Mission was not completed with just the constituting. That afternoon the new church met again and ordained their lay pastor to the gospel ministry.

As the time for Stacy and Sheila's furlough approached, they could look back on an amazingly productive few months with the Baptist Mission of Lesotho. Construction of the Mission house was underway and would be finished for their return in mid-1989. The first Baptist church was constituted and functioning with the first ordained minister. Plans were in place to purchase a large tent when the Housers returned. This tent would be used in evangelistic services in various villages and areas of the country. The other congregations were also prepared, with the help of the Maseru church, to continue functioning during this interim when there would be no Baptist missionaries in the country.

As we bade good-bye to the Housers at the end of their first trip to Maseru, we could not imagine how effective their months of work in Lesotho would be. We did know, though, that this was a wonderful missionary couple. Gratitude to God for preparing and calling them to Lesotho flooded our hearts. They were just the kind of colleagues we had prayed would come and help expand the witness and ministry of the Mission. Now they were here, and we were overjoyed and saddened. The sadness emanated from our disappointment that we would not have the privilege of working with them.

The character and spirit of these missionaries encouraged us. We and the intercessors did not understand why this first year had been as it had, but all of our spirits were lifted by the Housers' coming and the bright future which now lay ahead. Stacy and Sheila were going to have a blessed ministry in Lesotho.

With the Housers' trip behind us and our work with the film crew completed, we plunged into the final work of "mothballing" the Mission. Neither Nancy nor I was physically able for the nonstop work those last days required, but God made ways for us to get everything done. When I needed to move office furniture, but couldn't lift even the typewriter, men stopped by asking for day work. When I couldn't find storage space for the Mission equipment, the Holzes offered free storage in an extra room of theirs for as long as the Mission needed it. When it looked as if we would lose a great deal of money in reselling the new home appliances we had purchased, the insurance company that owned our apartment bought everything at our original purchase price. When my goal of solving the few outstanding Mission problems before we left seemed impossible, God resolved them, and the Housers had a clear road on which to begin their Lesotho journey.

When the dreaded last day finally arrived and I realized that actually leaving was going to be the toughest hurdle of all, God somehow gave the grace that enabled us to get in the truck and begin the trip. At the border post, I filled out the exit forms and remembered the first day we had rolled up to this same gate. Our very first minutes in the country had been difficult ones. Those and other difficulties had continued unabated throughout our entire time in Lesotho.

As we drove slowly out onto the narrow, rusty river bridge, I saw again the muddy waters of the Caledon below and remembered the swirling and clouded thoughts that had filled our minds as we entered Lesotho.

I looked ahead to the end of the bridge. It was close now and then we were across and out. Our last physical contact with Lesotho was broken.

With the second set of obligatory checks completed, we pulled away from the South African border post and began the climb up the hill out of the river valley. Before reaching the top, we pulled off the road and onto a level gravel overlook. We had one more responsibility to discharge. While the boys waited quietly in the truck, Nancy set up her video equipment. I clipped on a microphone and, at her signal, began to speak to the Missouri intercessors on what would be our last prayer video from Lesotho. Actually the spot on which I stood was not in Lesotho at all. We were already out of the country. Over my shoulders the intercessors had a panoramic view of Maseru and the mountains of Lesotho.

As I spoke to them about what had transpired in the last weeks and gave them new pressing prayer requests, I knew that the setting was speaking to them more loudly than my words. For reasons known only to God, Lesotho was now behind us. More important, though, as the intercessors looked at the scene on the video, they realized that I was very small in the picture, and Lesotho was very large. In another moment, we would step off the scene for good. What would be left was Lesotho. It would fill the screen. They would see that while Lesotho was now behind us, it was ever and more graphically before them. Their calling to this country and this Mission had not changed, except that the need for their ministry was more crucial now.

In these last words from us to ones who had paid a price to carve out a Mission here in this hidden corner of Africa, I affirmed them in their hidden and indispensable work. I exhorted them to deeper and fuller involvement and I thanked them. My friend and former seminary professor, T. W. Hunt, said in his book, *The Doctrine of Prayer:* "Prayer is the shaping force of history." As I looked into the video camera for the last time from Africa, I was conscious of the fact that I was speaking to history shapers. Lesotho was and would be different because of them. The kingdom of God was different because of them. History had been made by them. They were champions.

When the video was completed, I turned for one last look at Lesotho. I looked slowly at every visible building and street. I paused to look at the fields and the people. Most of all, I looked to the mountains. I wanted indelibly to imprint every aspect of this scene forever in my mind. After a long minute I gave up. It was no use. My eyes would not remain clear long enough to accomplish the task. I accepted the inevitable. Lesotho was to remain clouded and blurred for us. Only time might finally clear our vision of this country and this chapter of our lives.

It was time to turn and leave, but I couldn't bring myself to turn my back finally on this land. Then, at the edge of my consciousness, faintly from those mountains echoed familiar words. I had heard them before—on the eve of our entering this country. Now, here they were again. "Be strong and courageous! Do not tremble or be dismayed, for the Lord your God is with you wherever you go" (Josh. 1:9 NASB).

I turned around. We got into the truck and started up the hill and away from Lesotho. Toward the future.

We did not look back.

11

Passing the Torch

The neurosurgeon's tone was both serious and reassuring at the same time.

"I've reviewed all of your records and reports from the doctors in South Africa, as well as the results of the tests we've done here. Our tests confirm their diagnosis. You have damaged discs and vertebrae in both your neck and lower spine. I believe the condition in your neck is putting you at greatest risk, so I'd like to schedule surgery on it first. Would next week be all right with you?"

With my agreement, the surgeon stepped out of the examining room to make the call and schedule my surgery. Sitting alone, I reflected on the past few weeks. We had come home to a missionary house owned by Southwestern Baptist Theological Seminary in Fort Worth, Texas, and immediately made appointments with the appropriate specialists. Between periods of resting at the house, we had both gone through a series of medical tests and consultations. Nancy's rheumatologist had already confirmed her relapse and begun treatment for her lupus. My meeting on this particular day was to obtain the results of my tests. Now it was confirmed. I would have the surgery on my neck. A herniated disc would be removed and the two flanking vertebrae fused. A few months later, I would have a similar surgery on my lower back.

The surgeon returned, and I focused my attention on his instructions.

"I've made the arrangements," the surgeon stated as he handed me a slip of paper, "and here's the date and time that you need to be at the hospital for admission. I'll probably be able to perform the surgery the next morning."

After we returned to the mission house from the appointment, the first call we made was to Marilyn Coble, the state WMU prayer coordinator in Missouri. The Missouri intercessors were following closely our health developments. With the surgery decision finalized, we communicated the specifics to those who were waiting to pray. Marilyn had been anticipating our call and already had planned how she would use the telephone chain to spread the news. The maximum number of pray-ers would be ready and praying as I approached surgery. Marilyn was writing down the dates and times when abruptly she stopped speaking. I wondered what the pause meant when suddenly there came across the line an exclamation of what I took to be astonishment and praise.

"Randy!" Marilyn fairly shouted in a mixture of wonder and amazement. "I've been thinking and planning how I could notify the maximum number of people as quickly as possible so we could all be interceding for you as you go to surgery. Now I see that God has done it again. He is way out ahead of us. Do you know your hospitalization dates exactly overlay our state WMU annual meeting dates?"

I didn't, but I immediately saw again God's pattern of interaction with those who would take the ministry of intercession as theirs. His active answering always involved active advance preparation so His intercessors might accomplish His will. We were seeing it personally again.

Marilyn continued, "I've been working to gather pray-ers for you while God has already done far better than I ever could have. Over a thousand of us will be gathered and ready in Liberty, Missouri. Randy, listen to me, something's up."

As we completed our call, I had to agree. God was moving behind the scenes. Immediately, I felt more peace about the surgery and its outcome. Instead of wondering if my results might be similar to other patients I had met whose surgeries gave only limited relief from pain and immobility, I was assured. God was actively involved in this. I could rest in Him and the outcome He was preparing for me.

After settling into my room at the hospital the next week, I was given two injections which I was told would relax me in preparation for a myelogram. As the drugs took effect, I contrasted the myelogram with one I had several months earlier in Africa. There I had been laid on a metal table and without the benefit of either sedation or an anesthetic simply told, "Don't move." The doctor then inserted a needle into my spine and performed the procedure. I was thankful, as the orderly wheeled me to the radiology department, that I was back in the United States.

The myelogram was supposed to be a basic straightforward test that would provide the surgeon with definitive information he would need to perform the surgery. In my case the test was far from routine, and toward the end of the test I lost consciousness. Sometime later, I vaguely could hear people scrambling around the X-ray room hurriedly opening and closing drawers and cabinets. Then I heard the surgeon's voice instructing the others to watch me for cardiac arrest.

Because of the unexpected turn my test had taken, I was kept in the X-ray room for an extended period while another doctor monitored me. Finally, he and the surgeon were satisfied that I was fine. A nurse wheeled me into the waiting area where the surgeon would come to talk to me. I was expecting him to detail the damage as they had seen it and describe exactly what he was planning to do in surgery the next day. Instead, he brought a very different message.

"Mr. Sprinkle, this is extremely difficult to explain. In contrast to your previous x rays, myelogram, and MRI (magnetic resonance imaging), the myelogram this afternoon indicates a very different situation from the one you previously exhibited."

Since I was still not thinking clearly, I asked him what he meant.

In response he said, "We were going to remove a herni-ated disc that was causing your problems. Now, though, it is a perfectly normal, healthy disc."

I was still in the sedation fog, precluding my grasping the ramifications of his statement. Slowly, I worded anoth-er question.

"So, what does this mean for me now?"

"Well, we'll keep you overnight for observation and then tomorrow I'll release you and you can go home. In the morning when you feel better, I'll talk with you about options that may provide you with some additional relief."

After a night of deep sleep and a thorough discussion with the surgeon, I checked out of the hospital with a pre-scription for a lengthy period of physical therapy and treat-ment. Clearly, and unmistakably, God had intervened and healed the damaged disc in my neck. And, although I was not completely returned to my former health, I felt better already.

The morning after I returned to our mission house, I was home alone when the phone rang. I answered it and was met by silence. *Is this a prank call?* I thought.

Then, just as I was about to hang up, a woman's voice said, tentatively, "Randy?"

"Yes," I answered.

Another pause, and then a louder and more forceful reply, "What are *you* doing there?"

At this point, I thought I recognized the voice. "Marilyn, is that you?"

"Yes, it is, but why are you answering the phone? I was calling Nancy to find out how you came through your surgery yesterday."

I began to detail for Marilyn what had transpired at the hospital. She marveled as I talked about how God had worked on my behalf.

In the weeks and months that followed, we received numerous letters and personal descriptions of what occurred when Marilyn returned to the WMU annual meet-ing and stood before the assemblage. There were few dry eyes as she related what God had done for us in answer to their prayers. Gratitude and thanksgiving characterized the prayers of the women as they paused before God.

We were so grateful to God for His healing intervention in our lives. Later, though, we, along with many of these dedicated pray-ers, began to ask a question. *Why has it happened as it has?* God could have healed me in Africa just as easily as He had here in the States. Then we could have continued our ministry. Instead, He chose not to. We, alone, and in discussion with some of the intercessors, considered this question. The best answer we could give was found in His sovereign wisdom. He has His ultimate purposes that we often will not understand fully.

Back in Fort Worth, with the cause of my problems now removed, I began the therapy which, week-by-week, helped to lessen my symptoms. The inflammation in my spine reduced and my back strengthened. I was beginning to be able to straighten my legs again. Clearly, I was making progress, however, our recoveries were going to take an extended time. The Foreign Mission Board began to encourage us to plan for stateside employment. By the end of the summer, I accepted the call of the First Baptist Church of St. Joseph, Missouri, to become their associate pastor, and we officially went on a medical leave of absence with the Foreign Mission Board.

Through the summer as we were experiencing transition in our lives, the Housers were seeing their summer of accomplishments in Lesotho punctuated by a near-tragic event with an unseen prophetic aspect to it.

Their younger son Derek was born in April 1979. In December of that year, on the day that Stacy was to graduate from seminary, the Housers learned that Derek had hemophilia. Through proper care and treatment Derek had lived a normal life, and the Foreign Mission Board had commissioned them for missionary service. A condition of their assignment was that they be in an area where proper blood supplies and medical facilities were available if and when needed. The excellent medical care available in South Africa had met these criteria and the Housers had been assigned to the South African homeland of Bophuthatswana.

During the summer of their transitional work in Lesotho, a chilling development occurred. Medical officials discovered that 80 to 90 percent of the blood concentrate in

South Africa was contaminated with the HIV virus. The Foreign Mission Board's medical consultant worked quickly in the United States to locate the type of blood concentrate which Derek needed and air-expressed it to the Housers. Several weeks later as they left on furlough, Stacy and Sheila knew that they would have to make arrangements for a safe supply of the blood concentrate for Derek before they returned to Lesotho.

The Housers returned to Palacios, Texas, for furlough. In the fall of 1988, as they reveled in the renewal of friendships in Palacios and we were making new friends in St. Joseph, Alberta Gilpin was formulating a dramatic plan for the WMU annual meeting in the spring. Her letters of invitation to us and the Housers detailed the proposed meeting.

The 1989 meeting was planned for the southeastern Missouri town of Poplar Bluff. There, in the large sanctuary of the First Baptist Church, the women of Missouri WMU would experience personally the transition which God had already wrought in the Lesotho Mission. In a dramatic ceremony, the Sprinkles symbolically would pass the torch to the Housers, thus representing the end of one phase and the beginning of another. The work that the intercessors had done in establishing the Mission would take on new character as the Housers and other missionaries who would later join them developed and matured the ministry of the Baptist Mission of Lesotho.

Through the winter months we were encouraged both by the prospects of the spring meeting and by our improving health. We were excited.

WMU annual meeting, 1989, was going to be like no other Missouri had ever experienced.

12

Onward Until the Stars Appear

Winter was finally over. All around, in the final days of March, the world was filled with evidences of hope and new life. The encouragement of springtime was upon Missouri, and it was upon the women who had clung prayerfully to hope through the long, dark winter that was the first two years of life for the Baptist Mission of Lesotho.

Now less than three weeks remained before the spring meeting of Missouri WMU. In Poplar Bluff, the intercessors would participate in the formal completion of the inaugural period of the Missouri/Lesotho Mission endeavor. The questions and struggles that had characterized those first days of establishing a new Mission would be wrapped in a concluding ceremony.

The first chapter, as difficult as it had been, was over. A new surge of confidence would come with the sending of the Housers to take up the work in Lesotho. They would be the tangible evidence of God's active, ongoing involvement in the Lesotho Mission. We might not understand all of His ways, but surely we could never doubt again that He would answer. The Housers represented hope.

At home in St. Joseph, Nancy and I were experiencing a recurring rush of emotions that quickly settled into a predictable pattern. Each time we thought of the approaching meeting with its inevitably emotional conclusion, we were faced with the painful personal message that it would carry for us. When we passed the torch to Stacy and Sheila and symbolically to the other missionaries who would later join them we would also be performing our last active duty as Lesotho missionaries. The women in the audience would not know that our medical leave of absence was coming to an end. Despite our somewhat improved health, we and the Foreign Mission Board knew we would not be able to return to Africa.

For us, the thought of this reality brought waves of grief. We questioned ourselves, our actions, and our decisions until we were exhausted. Was there something we could have done differently? Could we have stayed longer? Had we done something to cause any of this difficulty and pain for the Mission and the Missouri intercessors? Always the sequence of questions led to the Housers and the evidence they were to us. For whatever the reasons, we were being led in a new direction and God was calling the Housers to take up the Lesotho task.

Each time that we arrived at this point, our grief was overwhelmed by thanksgiving. For us, as for the intercessors, Stacy and Sheila personified hope. They were God's answer. They were the future of the Mission. They were that one essential that the Mission needed to survive and to go forward. And so time and again, we gave thanks for them and what they represented.

We were glad, with just three weeks remaining, that we felt as we did. We were finally ready for the meeting, but not for the telephone call we were about to receive.

From the first moment I heard Alberta's familiar voice, I knew something was wrong. Stacy had called. Unknown to the Housers, a medical team from Houston had been trying to locate them. They had just located the Housers in Palacios and the message for them was devastating.

During Stacy's tenure as director of the camp at Palacios, Derek had been treated in a hemophilia program in Houston. Now, several years later, shocking news had been discovered. Seventy to 80 percent of the patients treated in that program during the years 1983 to 1985 were testing positive for the HIV virus. The medical team had been searching for the Housers because Derek had been treated there during that time.

Stacy and Sheila had immediately contacted the medical consultant at the Foreign Mission Board and over the next few days discussed with him what they should do. When they were at peace about their decision, they called Alberta to inform her. The high probability that Derek might eventually test HIV-positive, coupled with the difficulty of obtaining a safe blood supply in Africa, had forced them to a very painful decision. They would not be able to come to the annual meeting, and they would not be going to Lesotho. The Housers were resigning from foreign mission service.

Our initial response of heartache and empathy for Derek and his family mirrored Alberta's feelings. We struggled to express our emotions. Finally, near the end of the conversation, discussion turned briefly to what new plans needed to be formulated for the annual meeting. Of course, the scheduled passing of the torch could not happen. Beyond that, though, was another problem. After the ceremony, Stacy was to have preached the keynote message of the meeting. Alberta had not had time to decide what she should do about this. As we were concluding the call, she wondered aloud if someone from the Foreign Mission Board, possibly the area director for Eastern and Southern Africa, might be able to come and speak. I volunteered to call Richmond and check.

In my call to the Board, I learned that the area director was out of the country, but Zeb Moss, the associate director, was available and willing to come if Alberta desired. I relayed this to her and then promised my continuous prayer support as she struggled to finalize the necessary decisions.

Our praying for her in the days ahead came out of hearts that were clouded by confusion. We turned to God. What else could we do? It was impossible for us even to begin to understand what was going on with this missions effort and particularly with the missionaries who had come to be associated with it.

As I prayed for God to guide Alberta, I became aware that His answer was being given not only to her but to me. Despite my silent protests, I eventually accepted from Him that Alberta would not be calling Zeb but be calling me.

Thus, Alberta's call a few days later was not a surprise. "Randy, I believe you are the one to speak to the women. Would you accept responsibility for the message in the concluding session of the meeting?"

Even as I accepted, my impression was that I was more disturbed and confused than anyone else by the events of two years that had now culminated in this tragic situation for the Housers. I found solace in the lonely days of struggle that followed. God had made clear that He had chosen me for this critical moment. Based on that singular assurance, I was able to pray boldly. As I pled, I raised only one appeal: *Give the message I am to carry.*

When finally I left with friends on April 13, to begin the long drive across the state from the northwest corner where we lived to the southeast corner and Poplar Bluff, I was not going disappointed. I understood as the hours of driving passed that history was hinging on a moment very soon to arrive. I could have been anxious about what might transpire, but I was not. Actually, I could hardly wait for the moment. I knew what no one else knew. God had given His message.

Early the next morning in a motel room, Alberta and I met with the state WMU president, Norma Altis, and vice-president, Dawn Phillips. One issue remained unresolved. The women of the Missouri WMU did not yet know of the developments with the Housers and the changes that had been made in the annual meeting program. Now we had to decide how and when and by whom the women would be told. All of us relived the trauma we had experienced upon hearing the Housers' news. We knew these committed women were coming from across the state, filled with anticipation of seeing in person the answers to their prayers and experiencing this dramatic moment in their Lesotho pilgrimage. Because of their heightened expectations for these days, their shock and grief might be greater than ours had been.

We talked and we prayed. We concluded that Alberta, as state director, must bring the sad news. She would do so immediately after the opening session convened.

The shock and sorrow that day were as we had anticipated. With sensitivity, Alberta reported the developments in the lives of the Houser family and informed the women that they would not be at the annual meeting as planned. Then she explained that in order to care for Derek and to provide the safest environment for him, the Housers were resigning from the Foreign Mission Board and would not be going to Lesotho.

A thousand eager women were listening. They were stunned. Alberta's words burst upon them. When she finished speaking, there was silence, then sobbing.

Other business was transacted that afternoon, though most of us remember none of it.

Slowly, the old nagging question began to surface in minds again. Why, when we have been praying as never before, do things continue to worsen?

Gratefully, these committed servants did not give much time to considering this difficult question. Instead, they allowed themselves and their thoughts to be driven by another emotion. First pulsing and then swelling through the hours of that meeting was the powerful emotion of love. We didn't recognize its full significance or what God was about to do through it, but before the meeting concluded, that love was to win a great victory.

Because the Housers were not present at the meeting, I stood at the Lesotho booth in the missionary mall. There, through the two days of the meeting, I spoke to many of the women and heard the expressions of their deepest distresses regarding the Missouri/Lesotho partnership.

Some said, "It's too bad how things have worked out."

Others expressed, "It was a good idea, but apparently it wasn't God's will."

Still others felt, "Beginning the Mission and the partnership was right, but the circumstances now show that it's time to give them up."

The most frequent expression was, "I just don't understand." But in spite of their confusion, overwhelmingly, these women were unwilling to give up. They couldn't understand what was happening. They were struggling—but they weren't finished.

During the 24 hours that elapsed between the announcement of the developments with the Housers and the concluding session of the annual meeting, a critical realization began to dawn upon us. Our attention had been focused on the unstaffed Mission and the young congregations in Lesotho which were in potential peril. We had prayed fervently for God to call someone to fill the vital need. When the Housers were called out, they were to us His answer. When they were removed, we were shocked and confused. We had been seeing the situation from our perspective. Now we saw it from God's. All along we had thought that we needed the Housers. Now we saw that they needed us.

God, in love, had grafted them into the Missouri prayer tree, not to meet the needs in Lesotho, but because His love needed a channel to love the Housers and to meet their needs. To their great credit, the Missouri intercessors saw this, and from them poured such prayers birthed by love as can hardly be imagined.

As we came to the closing session of the meeting and the future that would be decided there, I did not know that the Enemy's strategy to deal a deathblow to the Lesotho Mission and its prayer foundation contained this one fatal flaw: he had failed to take into account the power of love.

I did know, as I stood before the women, that much questioning was going on both at the Foreign Mission Board and in the Missouri WMU regarding the prayer partnership and whether the Baptist Mission of Lesotho should be continued. I also knew, as I asked the women to open their Bibles to the sixth chapter of Ephesians, that it was not an exaggeration to think that the future of the Mission and the prayer partnership likely hung on this hour. Asking them to follow with me, I read these words from verses 10 -13:

"Finally, be strong in the Lord, and in the strength of His might. Put on the full armor of God, that you may be able to stand firm against the schemes of the devil. For our struggle is not against flesh and blood, but against the rulers, against the powers, against the world forces of this darkness, against the spiritual forces of wickedness in the heavenly places. Therefore, take up the full armor of God, that you may be able to resist in the evil day, and having done everything, to stand firm" (NASB).

I finished reading. Hundreds of faces looked to me for a

word. Speaking to friends, I walked them back to the birth of this partnership. We had to remember that God had initiated it. He had been the foundational rock on which we had taken the first step of this pilgrimage. He was the author and overseer of all that we were about, then and now. That understanding, and our commitment to follow, could not change now.

We rehearsed the great victories we had seen in two years. We acknowledged His faithfulness and power brought to earth, brought to Lesotho, by our intercessions. No one must miss, as I came to the bog of confusion in which we were now mired, that God had been present and active in every day of His prayer partnership.

With this preface set, I addressed the issue at the front of everyone's mind: Why, if God has been in all that we were doing, and why, if we were faithfully praying as He has commanded us, are the missionaries that He has called being pulled out and laid aside? Their lives are desperately needed in Lesotho and in the ministry there. We know how hard it is to get missionaries and how long it takes for them to become proficient in the language and culture of a country. We know without them the Mission cannot last. Surely something is wrong, in us or in our praying or in our understanding of God's will, when first the Sprinkles and now the Housers are struck down.

Sitting before me were women of all ages. To them, I could say, "I know by looking at you that in World War II, Korea, or Vietnam, many of you experienced personally what it is to lose beloved sons and husbands and fathers to the violence of battle. We know the costs of earthly war. We are surprised, though, by the costs of spiritual war.

"Ladies, fellow soldiers, we are at war. In the balance hangs a nation, small but vital, mostly unknown to the world, but known in love to God and us. We, all of us as Missouri Baptists, were chosen as the expeditionary force for the new front that our Commander-in-Chief decided to open in Lesotho. We obeyed orders and began to move. A foothold was established. Progress was made. But now, in the losing of frontline troops, we have forgotten one thing, and it has brought the ultimate success of the campaign into serious question.

"Ladies, we must never forget: In war, there are going to be casualties.

"Furthermore, our Enemy, the devil, is delighted by the present situation. He sees this prayer partnership, the first ever formed to birth a new Mission, now on the verge of death. He already has prepared the tombstone that he intends to erect over the grave of this once promising endeavor. And if it should die, I know the epitaph he has already chosen to write upon that stone."

I was struggling with control of my voice as I measured the next words. "That epitaph will read, For They Wrestled Not."

If this Mission and this partnership were to die, it would happen because we were no longer willing to struggle.

Then came from the exploding fire within me with such force and volume that the reverberations shocked even me, these words: "But by God's grace, we shall not let it be!"

After a ringing period of silence, I continued. "In these past days, since the word of the Housers' resignation came, I have searched the heart of God to know if this development spelled the end to all that we have been about, together, on mission. The answer I have to give to you today is no answer at all. There has been no word. Heaven has been silent.

"And the message I understand in that silence is this: No orders have been rescinded. No directions have been changed. Our commission stands!"

The organist began to play softly. Holding aloft a leather-bound book I spoke these concluding words.

"In this book is the original prayer covenant of the partnership. In this book the first intercessors sealed with their signatures their commitment to enter upon this prayer/missions journey. Today we stand at a historic moment. That which we began under God is in danger of destruction. The battle has been more costly than we ever imagined. The struggle is going to be longer and more difficult than we had originally thought.

"God has made plain to us His desire. Our commission is unchanged. Our service is essential. The future of the Baptist Mission of Lesotho is in our hands. God waits.

"There will be no invitation hymn today. There will not even be a hymn of commitment. Today, this moment, there can be only a *call to arms.*

"Women here at the front stand with pages lifted from this very book. If you will answer the call, come, sign, and seal your commitment. I will replace the pages in this book after this meeting. Now, though, is the time to decide. We will sing. I will wait."

As I stood, the words of the chosen hymn began to rise in that sanctuary.

Onward, Christian soldiers,
Marching as to war,
With the cross of Jesus
Going on before!
Christ, the royal Master,
Leads against the foe;
Forward into battle,
See His banner go![1]

Standing and waiting, I knew I watched not alone. God and a host of those on both sides of the battle waited to see what the choice of the warriors would be. Neither I nor they had long to wait.

Love had earlier moved the confusion and questions off center stage and focused our attention on people in need. Now love welled up in the hearts of these intercessors standing face-to-face with decision.

I had wondered who the first woman might be to step out and accept the charge. I tell you today, there was no first woman. From the initial strains of that mighty Christian battle hymn, the whole sanctuary seemed to be in motion. In every quarter there was no hesitation. God's will in Lesotho must be done. These were the women who were to do it. They were willing. And love—love for God and love for the Basotho—provided the motivation. Every aisle of that great church filled with long lines of intercessors.

Hudson Taylor, the pioneering China missionary, once said, "There are three phases in most great tasks undertaken for God . . . impossible, difficult, done."

That hour soldiers saw again the great task set before them.

That hour intercessors accepted the cost of their commission.

That hour a future in jeopardy became a future secured.

That hour love broke through.

That hour in Missouri, it was done.

[1]"Onward, Christian Soldiers" (*Baptist Hymnal*).

13

The Story Continues

From the meeting in Poplar Bluff in April 1989, the intercessors went back to their homes and to their prayer posts.

The summer of that year was characterized by two things: faithful intercession and divine silence. The women persevered with a new hope and joy that sprung out of the deepened love-bond God had formed in them with the people of Lesotho. These were changed women, and this was a changed prayer partnership. Even if they were not hearing of the answers to their prayers, they *knew* God was hearing and answering.

One of the daily prayer requests during those months of summer was again for missionaries to be sent to Lesotho. Seemingly, God only communicated His response to this prayer to one person. That person was area director for Eastern and Southern Africa, John Faulkner.

In September John and his wife, Ann, went to visit one of the mission stations in Kenya. There they stayed with missionaries Wayne and Alice McMillian. One day John went with Wayne to visit a new church that he had helped start. After the service held under a tree, John and Wayne began the drive back to the house. As they drove, John, surprisingly, began to talk not about the work in Kenya but about work in a country named Lesotho. He told Wayne about the Mission's short history, about the Sprinkles and the Housers and their problems, and about the prayer partnership. Then he said, "I really need somebody there. In fact, I needed somebody there yesterday."

"John," Wayne ventured, "are you talking to me about going there?"

"Wayne, I can't ask you to go; but if you feel called to go there, please let me know. I'm going to leave a copy of the job description for the Lesotho position with you. Since I'm preparing to leave for the States to attend the next Board meeting, I must have an answer from you and Alice within a week."

After the Faulkners left, Wayne and Alice began to ask God if this was His will for them. At first, they were reluctant to consider a move to southern Africa because of the problems in South Africa; but by Thursday of that week they knew. God was calling them to Lesotho.

Their older daughter Cheri, then 13, was away at boarding school outside of Nairobi. They did not want to finalize the decision without discussing it with her. On Friday they drove to Cheri's school and told her about the move they were considering. Cheri's response was, "Whatever you think is right is fine with me." Then the McMillians drove to John Faulkner's office in Nairobi and told him they were ready to transfer to Lesotho.

In October John called me from Richmond, Virginia, to say that missionaries in Kenya had just been approved by the Board for transfer to Lesotho. We immediately spread the word in Missouri, and the rejoicing began.

The McMillians learned of the approval of their transfer about the first of November 1989. During the next month, they worked hard to sell most of their belongings in preparation for the move. Toward the end of that month, when pressures and stresses were building, a package arrived. It was from James Westmoreland at the Baptist International Missions office in Johannesburg. The McMillians were puzzled as they opened the parcel. They had not ordered anything. What a surprise was theirs when inside they found more than 100 letters from intercessors in Missouri.

James could have held the letters until they arrived, but he felt they needed this mail in Kenya now, rather than later in South Africa. He was right. The McMillians were overcome by the love expressed for them by the Missourians. The prayer requests in the letters were specifically relevant to their exact needs and concerns.

The McMillians arrived in southern Africa in December and soon moved to Lesotho. The missionary home which the Housers had seen built awaited them, and they were able to move right in.

The tenor of life and work in Lesotho has not changed significantly since the earliest days of the Mission. Since the McMillians did not have a checking account in Maseru, they took to Lesotho all of the money from the sale of their things in Kenya. Almost immediately, their home was burglarized and all of their funds stolen. The Missouri WMU not only prayed for the McMillians during this time, but also raised a special offering and sent it to help cover their loss.

They eventually got settled in their ministry and began developing the existing congregations, while starting new ones as well.

Through the early months of 1991, a special prayer concern was for a Southern Baptist missionary doctor for Lesotho. By mid-1991 this request was answered. Ron and Gloria Murff moved from Rwanda and began work in Lesotho. Ron serves as a flying doctor, utilizing the services of the pilots and planes of Mission Aviation Fellowship. He is doing both medical and church development work in the remote villages of the mountains.

One more example illustrates God's ongoing work, cooperating with the intercessors to meet the needs of the Mission and the missionaries in Lesotho. In May 1991 Fred Allen, a retired sailor and deacon at First Baptist Church of St. Joseph, Missouri, was watching a television news broadcast when it was announced that a coup had taken place in Lesotho and rioting and burning had broken out. Fred immediately picked up his phone and called me with the news. I went to my home and watched the next news report. There was no mention of Lesotho. That evening I watched the broadcast again, as well as the network news. Again, no mention of Lesotho. I called Fred back to confirm that he indeed had understood the news report correctly. He was positive of what he had reported to me. Based on that we began to spread the news to the Missouri intercessors. Immediate prayer was begun for the missionaries and the Basotho.

The next day I called the Foreign Mission Board to learn if they had any additional information I could relay to the intercessors. I was amazed by what I learned. The Foreign Mission Board knew nothing of the coup and the civil unrest.

Later, in correspondence with the McMillians, we learned what had transpired during those terrifying days. Wayne had been out of the country attending a conference when the unrest began. Alice was home alone with their two daughters. The rioting broke out over the murder of a woman in a store. Immediately, tension in the country exploded. For the next several nights, there was burning and looting. Violence caused widespread injuries and deaths. During this entire period, Alice remained in the house with her children. Not once were they threatened or in any imminent danger.

When she felt most afraid, God sent another missionary couple to her home. Unable to reach their own home because of the rioting, they decided to stop at the McMillians'. The couple stayed with Alice and the girls for the next few days. Alice did not know Missourians knew what was happening and had been praying for them continuously until Alberta Gilpin reached her by phone. That call, with its assurance that Missouri was aware and interceding, was the watershed for Alice. She understood why they had been perfectly protected.

After this episode I marveled again at God's working with His co-laborers. They intercede, and He bestows His grace throughout the world. The reason the Foreign Mission Board knew nothing about the coup and the rioting was not that their communications network was faulty. Actually, it is quite superior; immediately upon receiving word of the situation in Lesotho, they sprang into action and provided excellent assistance and information. The real reason the Board did not learn first of the dangerous situation in Lesotho was that God first notified the intercessors. They were on the front line.

And they still are.

The last days of 1993 brought further good word for Lesotho. Newly-appointed missionaries Clif and Mary Sue Jones along with their young children, Natalie and Samuel, completed training at the Missionary Learning Center near Richmond, Virginia. They began their church development work in Lesotho in early 1994.

Also Charles and Glenda Middleton, 25-year veterans of ministry in Malawi and Transkei, transferred to Lesotho to work in church development. They served productively together until September 22, 1995, when tragedy struck. While traveling to a missions prayer retreat in neighboring South Africa, Glenda was killed in a car accident. Charles is presently (mid-1996) on leave in the United States.

Wayne and Alice McMillian, after a very productive first term, took furlough and then an extended leave of absence. After much prayer, they returned to Kenya where they are again serving.

The Murffs were very effective in their medical and evangelistic ministries. They completed their term of service in Lesotho and are currently on leave of absence in the United States.

The Housers, after serving in a pastorate, are now at Baylor University where Stacy is on the staff. Andrew and Derek are healthy, active teenagers and Derek continues to test HIV-negative.

The Sprinkles now reside in Richmond, Virginia, where Randy serves as director of the Foreign Mission Board's International Prayer Strategy Office.

The story of the Missouri/Lesotho Prayer Partnership continues, just as does the Story of which it is a small part.

The Son Prince will be coming back again, maybe soon. Until then, He seeks partners who will labor with Him for the advance of God's kingdom on earth, partners who will intercede until the stars appear.

Southern Baptist churches interested in prayer partnerships can call the International Prayer Strategy Office toll-free at 1 (888) 462-7729 for information.